Helsingborg

The continent starts here

This book is produced by the City of Helsingborg
in cooperation with Liljedahl Blå

This book is produced by the City of Helsingborg
in cooperation with Liljedahl Blå

Editor: Anders Donelius
Account Management: Bengt Liljedahl
Editorial Board: Elisabeth Aldstedt, Ole Andersson, Peter Danielsson, Anders Donelius, Lars Johansson, Bengt Liljedahl, Noushin Nadjafi, Ola Thufvesson, Sten-Åke Tjärnlund
Art Direction: Clas Håkansson
Final art: Karolina Jönsson
Translation: Sven H.E. Borei
Printing and reproduction: Göteborgstryckeriet, Mölndal 2007

ISBN 978-91-975711-4-2

Next page: The inner harbour, located right downtown, was built allready in the 1860s.

SUNDBUSS PERNILLE

Preface

Labelling Helsingborg is hard. Not because there isn't a lot to praise here. As you can read in this book, the problem is rather an overabundance.

So what is it that makes Helsingborg so special? The answer is that it depends on whom you ask. Those who share their special relationship with the city here range from academics, entrepreneurs and branding experts to immigrants, cultural personalities and journalists.

It is my wish that this book will serve as an appetizer – nay a magnet to draw you to the Pearl of the Sound, as Helsingborg is called. And if you already live here, the book can be an entertaining inspiration about our own city. You'll find useful facts, lovely pictures and interesting opinions about such facets as culture, sports and city history.

These pages glow with the warm feelings Helsingborgians hold for their city. Few cities can boast of such a cadre of goodwill ambassadors.

You are most welcome to visit our Pearl, for only by coming here, can you check if we are right about Helsingborg!

Peter Danielsson
Chairman of the Municipal Executive Committee

UNO

The Spirit of Helsingborg

By Noushin Nadjafi
Helsingborgian and entrepreneur

Helsingborg is more than the sea and the shore ridge; it is also people like Johan Jacob Döbelius, Carlos Zoéga and Henry Dunker. It would seem that the city has always owned the power to draw strangers to it from different parts of the world and make them its eternal citizens. Is it merely a coincidence or is there something else, a spirit – a Helsingborgian spirit?

What a lovely thought!

Perhaps that soul lies in its lack of prejudice, perhaps in its interest in the unknown. Maybe that soul is what attracts skilful businessmen and women from far and wide to Helsingborg, making of it the highest ranked entrepreneurial city in Sweden. If that is so, then we must nurture that heritage in the best way possible. For nothing arises from nowhere and nothing lasts forever.

Survey after survey has shown that Helsingborg is a city with proud, prospering residents. Simply put, people feel at home here, regardless of where they were born. Still, we must not be satisfied until all Helsingborgians feel a part of their city. Only then have we succeeded completely.

This book offers proof that we are on the right path.

Previous page:
Folk-life on Bruksgatan.

The continent starts here

By Ola Thufvesson
PhD in social geography, senior lecturer at Campus Helsingborg

As during the 1980s some Scanian ferry ports sold themselves as "the gate to the continent", Helsingborg went a step further. At the city approaches signs were put up saying. "The continent starts here".

Obviously Helsingborg is part of Sweden and anyone who looks at a map can see that Skåne is most certainly part of the Scandinavian Peninsula. To top it off, the latter is actually named after Skåne. Even so, everyone who visits or moves in says that Helsingborg is not a run-of-the-mill Swedish municipal capital. Some point to the many promenade streets, the shops and street cafés; others are charmed by the constantly present water, the beaches downtown and that another country waits but twenty minutes west by ferry. Then there are those who insist that the rocks and the houses are not like those at home or that Helsingborg feels more like a city than what they had expected. Quite often the concept 'continental' is used when these visitors and 'immigrants' try to describe the city in one word.

This chapter will explore that diffuse feeling that Helsingborg does not follow the standard Swedish guidelines for cities. So what makes us dare to call Helsingborg a continental city?

Previous page:
Helsingborg is a compact city. At the bottom of the picture is the Olympia football pitch, followed by Olympia's Art Deco district, Kärnan castle, downtown, Öresund and finally Denmark with Helsingör.

The physical site

Three major natural qualities join forces to make the place where Helsingborg has grown a very difficult factor to copy.

First is the twenty to forty metre high plateau called Landborgen that traverses the whole city. This abrasion cliff stands parallel to and sometimes only a block away from the second natural component, the Öresund Sound. This combination of height and sea grants the city a host of attractive lookout localities. Whoever looks west spots Denmark a seeming stone's throw away. Looking southwest reveals Ven Island and the silhouettes of large cities. Northwards the narrow Sound opens up into the broad Kattegatt.

The combination of height and sea is made perfect by the sun as the third quality component. Since Helsingborg's coastline faces west, the sun shines on the shore walks and shore ridge from the most attractive quarter. On summer evenings, Helsingborgians can watch the sun descend into the Kattegatt horizon.

The sheep's walks at Tinkarp can give you the feel of how Helsingborg looked before it was built up. No other Scanian cities can boast of owning such a natural situation: Malmö without the city would have been a windblown sandbank set in a flat coastal landscape; were Lund not there, the site would be only a sloping field; and Kristianstad without its urban spread a swamp.

View from the popular shore ridge promenade placed higher than the downtown roof ridges.

At the Tinkarpshagen near Sofiero you can get a good idea of how Helsingborg looked before the city itself was founded.

The strategic location

Today people mostly see the combination of a high ridge near the sea as being attractive, but it was neither real estate dealers nor tourist guides who first discovered the place where Helsingborg would eventually grow. A high coast line by the narrowest part (3.7 km) along the sailing route between Kattegatt Bay of the North Sea and the Baltic was a bit too interesting to leave as a sheep pasture. Both commercial and military minds grasped this early on. Helsingborg is usually counted as one of the oldest Nordic cities, even if its birthdate is only set at May 21, 1085, because that is the date when the city is mentioned in a royal deed of gift.

Located as it was in the most central part of the Danish kingdom, Helsingborg became an important city in the Middle Ages. Its wealth was based on trade and the herring. A castle was built to defend it and to administer the county. In addition to the castle itself, the city's more monumental medieval buildings were a monastery and several churches.

Downtown Helsingborg still has its medieval street network. Narrow streets connected by meandering alleys have proven perfect for modern strolling. An excellent pedestrian street should be narrow enough to let the walker see the display windows on both sides simultaneously. It should even turn a bit so that more windows are exposed. Most cities in central Sweden have had a clear ambition to straighten and broaden the medieval streets, even as early as the 1600s. This was done to create order and to prevent fires, but resulted at the same time in greater predictability and less cosy avenues.

Unfortunately all that is left of the medieval monumentality is the Maria Church and the old keep of the castle, called Kärnan. The monastery and the other churches disappeared during the reformation in the 1500s. During the many wars between Denmark and Sweden in the 1600s, Helsingborg changed hands many times. Each shift was hard on the residents and their buildings. When the wars finally ended in 1710 not many of the older houses were still standing and of the castle, only the Kärnan keep remained.

One of the oldest pictures of Helsingborg is of a small, medieval city by the shore below the well-fortified castle.

The period between the wars and industrialism are usually described with allusions to Sleeping Beauty. Having once stood in the middle of Denmark, the city was now a small, unimportant town in Sweden's outskirts. Still, it is worth remembering that after Stockholm, the most important cities in Sweden during the 1700s were Göteborg, Norrköping and Karlskrona, all with around 10 000 residents.

The double nationalities

The small, pre-industrial city is today best preserved in the blocks around Södra Storgatan, Strömgränden and Tycho Brahes Place.

Springpostgränden Alley – the houses on the right are well-preserved remnants of the small pre-industrial city of Helsingborg.

Helsingborg is unique in that its twin-city Helsingör made it through the 17th century wars rather intact. Kronborg, Europe's best-preserved Renaissance palace, is found there, along with more than twenty blocks of older buildings. The number of half-timbered houses in central Helsingör is so numerous no one has counted them.

Helsingör is still part of Denmark. Over the years, having a national boundary between the two halves of the city district has meant quite

NETOPTIK
synoptik
THIELE
BANK
TILBUD
vin & sprit
EKSTRA PRIS

Commerce and folk-life on Helsingör's main street.

some problems over the years. But there are advantages – there has always been something better, tastier, more fun and cheaper to find on the other side. Thus what is Danish in Helsingborg is not only some medieval traces that gradually fade over time. Rather it is something most vital that is replenished daily, leaving impressions for both residents and visitors.

Helsingborg does indeed grace the outskirts of the continent. It takes only a thirty minute drive north on E4 to reach the start of the interconnected evergreen forest that covers Scandinavia up to the alpine regions with only a few breaks.

Entrepreneurial spirit

In the mid-1800s a number of political and technological changes occurred that would contribute to radical societal changes in Sweden. The two-chamber parliament, freedom of trade and religion, public schools, steam engines, railways and the telegraph are examples of these novelties that transformed a poor, agrarian country to a modern, industrial nation. Obviously Helsingborg was in no way a unique part of this development, but few places were as strongly affected.

One defining measure of urban expansion is population. Between 1870 and 1930, Helsingborg grew from 4 140 to 55 889, making the city the fifth largest in Sweden for a few decades in the mid-1900s. The percentage population growth from that time forwards has been somewhat more moderate. In actual numbers, we are talking about around 1 000 more Helsingborgians each year that passes, reaching 124 000 in 2007 who live in the Helsingborg Municipality.

There are a number of reasons why just Helsingborg has grown so quickly during the industrial period. One is the old strategic location that once more can be used. The city is located at a crossroad of several larger transport ways. At first it was mainly shipping, but the pattern was rapidly reinforced with railways and major roads.

Another factor is the entrepreneurial climate. Helsingborg became a sort of lilliputian America where energetic persons from near and far could start and develop companies. The results were all that counted, not one's family connections or that the business area was one of the

Industrial dynamics have fitted this small, widespread Scanian merchant city with grand, European big-city style fashionable streets. The picture shows Järnvägsgatan – Railway Street.

usual ones. Strong entrepreneurs competed and stimulated each other, while fully understanding the benefit of collaboration for the good of the city. Helsingborg is still a typical business city with comparable many companies in many different fields and a large percentage of the population in private employment. The city is one of the largest in the country and is often ranked high in various studies of business climate. However, as in all larger Swedish cities, various governments are the dominating employers.

If you draw two circles with a radius of 30, respective 60 km from central Helsingborg, you'll see how close the Öresund towns are to each other. The inner circle corresponds for the most part to the city's functional and mental metro region.

A well-populated region

Yet another vital factor in Helsingborg's strong growth and active cityscape is the richly populated vicinity in which it lies. When the overflow countryside population moved into the cities, Helsingborg and many Scanian cities with it had many eager to move in the immediate area. While it was tough to change to being an industrial worker, many Scanian natives did not have far to go, counted in kilometres.

Today Helsingborg lies in a well-populated part of the region. There are more than three hundred thousand persons living within 30 kilometres of city hall, most of whom consider Helsingborg as their somewhat larger central neighbouring town. Should that radius be stretched to the 60 kilometres that are a rather normal distance to the nearest city for most Swedes, the total population rises to more than two million. This is the Öresund Region that Helsingborg is a part of.

After Copenhagen and Malmö, Helsingborg is the largest town in that region. The cities all compete with and complement each other.

Ever since the inauguration of the Öresund Bridge in 2000, this exchange between the cities has increased greatly. Planners at the Skåne Traffic Authority work hard to acquire more train sets and schedule more departures to serve the increased commuter demand in the region.

The street life in the cityscape is not only dependent on having many people pass through or commute to Helsingborg. The town's many entrepreneurs have long made it clear that the large number of persons who can get to the city rather quickly are necessary to its advanced corporate services, exciting profile shops, individualistic cafés and top-class restaurants. Nor could the city's rich cultural life have survived without the added audience from the densely populated neighbouring municipalities.

In other words, Helsingborg's range of typical metropolitan activities is larger than in other Swedish municipalities of the same size. Places such as Uppsala and Linköping do have greater populations, but by counting the actual, functional trading area another, fully explanatory picture emerges. A city like Uppsala lies in the shadow of Stockholm. This means that it is not profitable to operate many kinds of activities in Uppsala in spite of its population of 183 000, since it is

Commuters in the combined railway, bus and ferry terminal Knutpunkten. The city's labour market is more and more integrated into the Öresund Region.

The Eneborg district is an example of the massive, European big-city blocks of the industrial age.

all too easy for the residents to travel to the capital. Had Skåne still been politically Danish, the Scanian cities would most likely have found themselves in the shadow of Copenhagen in much the same way.

A very local city

Helsingborg is considered a comparably handsome, well-preserved city. This is in much due to factors that already have been discussed, such as the location and the varied choice available. Another factor is the population development. In Sweden there is a clear connection between when cities have gone through expansion and how the cityscape appears. As was described above, Helsingborg had a very strong growth period in the late 1800s and that the city's population in 1930 was just under 56 000 souls. At that time, only Stockholm, Göteborg, Malmö and Norrköping were larger. That same year Uppsala had 30 000 residents and Linköping 29 000. The reason that 1930 is used as a key year is that it was around then that Sweden stopped building traditional urban settings with streets and city blocks. This was followed by an orientation to the suburban areas in accordance with the theories of functionalism. Cities that have grown a lot after that year have many areas from the 'modern' period.

Typical, older Scanian buildings in the Wilson Park district (at top) and on Råå.

A flat country, Skåne is part of the northwest European brick district. Thus there was a plentiful access to bricks at reasonable prices and the houses were solidly built. In many cities of central Sweden, the houses were mainly low and of wood. During the big demolition period during the 1960s, the wooden structures went first and brick-built Helsingborg survived comparably intact.

Post-1930s districts are in much very pleasant and well-built housing areas. The reason that it is good for a city to have a very traditional environment is not about the quality of living, but the quality of the city itself. Traditional block cities offer a rich aesthetic variation, where the land is well used and it is easy to orient. The system with streets and blocks also provides many possible localisations for shops and eateries.

Aerial photograph of the Tågaborg district. The much discussed, neo-modernistic buildings at the Norra Hamnen can be seen just below the park below the shore ridge.

Helsingborg has a large inner city. The city blocks start far up on Tågaborg and stretch all the way to the Söder district and Högaborg. There are also many, city-like areas with older housing that once lay far outside the central area and which the city has since incorporated and grown out to. The old fishing hamlet Råå is an example of such a town within the city. Other examples are Ramlösa,Wilson Park and Planteringen.

After 1930, Helsingborg continued to be a city with high architectural ambitions. The concert hall from 1932 and the large expositions in 1955 and 1999 are some of the best examples of this. For the last decade or so Helsingborg has been one of the most conspicuous cities in the country when it comes to creating new, modern city districts using thousand-year old, traditional city principles.

As this chapter has shown, the continental feel of Helsingborg can be explained both by geology and by a centuries-old history. In a manner of speaking, the city has received much of the continental free of charge. Still, it is also apparent that the city's residents have been and are skilled stewards and developers of their continental heritage both through their long-term visions and in their daily actions.

Sweden's Riviera

By Tomas Polvall
Freelance journalist and lecturer

Everywhere Helsingborg is lovely! You experience most of it in the best way by walking, but it is possible to come by car on the E4. As you approach the Sound it is called Hälsovägen – Health Road. At that point the road meanders in a ravine between two parks. The verdant verges rising into the Öresundsparken and Vikingsbergsparken are so steep that for a moment the traveller can wonder if the world has disappeared. It has! When it reappears again after the last curve, it is a shock, a beauty shock. The sea between the white buildings housing a concert hall and a theatre rise with such power that the only response is to brake and enjoy as long as possible. If the light at Henry Dunker Place turns red, you can see the blue between the buildings and wonder if a city can come any closer to the water. And not only here, for the sea pushes far into the city everywhere – the City Hall, squares like Stortorget, Hamntorget and Sundstorget are but a stone's throw from the Sound, as are many, many apartment houses.

All these hills

Hälsovägen is but one of many hills running to the sea. It is also possible to pedal a bike full speed down Halalid while thinking that no better way to reach the beach exists. But you'd be wrong. For Tinkarpsbacken is city-best on two wheels. At one time I lived in Helsingborg and bicycled to and from my job in Höganäs. Coming home Tinkarpsbacken was my speed dream. But the getting there was also a dream, cycling along the sea. The Stockholm journalist and author Jan Olof Olsson, best known as Jolo, also has had pleasure riding the coast road north of Helsingborg:

Previous page:
A summer day at Fria Bad.

"Of all roads these in north-western Skåne are almost the most pleasant in the country, in Europe, perhaps in the world. They meander so charmingly, be it by car, bicycle or on foot. The heat of the plain is eased at just the right moment by the sweet coolness of a beech copse or the somewhat harsher cold of an evergreen wood. And without warning, the sea appears, a lovely glimpse between two hillocks."

These hillocks lie between Kulla Gunnarstorp and Laröd. With good shape and lots of will, it is possible to cycle up and down the camel's back, as they are called, without even shifting down. Then the road meanders through Laröd and past Sofiero before gaining Tinkarpsbacken. Down you can ride as fast as the wind and more until you meet the tangy fragrance of seaweed just before the road levels onto Drottninggatan.

Bicycles and cars are OK, but cities should be experienced on foot. The handsome march of ocean views begins at Sofiero, continues through Pålsjö Woods and on all the way to Kärnan. Best is to keep going all the way to Ramlösa. In summertime and sun you can take the bus to Sofiero and enjoy breakfast with a royal view before starting your hike downtown.

Hälsovägen meanders down from north to the city centre. On reaching the last curve, the sea appears between the city theatre and the concert hall.

Nicandersgatan in the Tågaborg district is one of many streets that end abruptly at the edge of the shore ridge.

Personal favourites

Naturally those of us who have grown up here and learned to explore the town on foot have personal favourites. Which depends on where we lived and what we like. On calm, boiling summer days Nicandersgatan can't be beat. Since I lived just around the corner for several years, I have often wandered down the small, charming street.

Though habit often erases moments of beauty, I will never forget Nicandersgatan. Even before it has begun, it swings sharply right. Ten metres on, it turns left. That short straight fills my body with joy and yearning – I know what is coming and am never disappointed. The shadow of a lamppost falls like a boom over the street, making it natural to slow up a bit to feel the rising expectation. Sorrento echoes in my mind for it is the dream of Italy that is attained in Helsingborg. All of the Sound lies open to the gaze of the wanderer.

Here the world lies open and inviting, though I will not go so far. Here I never yearn to leave. You just cannot yearn to leave such an experience; still, when the sun hangs like a welder's torch over Kron-

People in bathrobes are a common sight in Helsingborg – at least during the summer!

Winter bathing is a popular Helsingborg diversion.

borg, the journey towards the sea must continue. Down the stairs to Margareta Place, through the park, over Drottninggatan and on past Gröningen – and to the beach of your choice: Tropical Beach, Gröningen, Kallis, Fria Bad or Pålsjö.

Summertime 2007 Gröningen has been given a wooden terrace by the beach and new quays – all you have to do is jump in and swim. Summer seas exist for swimming. When I swim, I am a swimmer. What I am on shore is unimportant. I don't even think about it. When I swim, I swim. As the summer passes, the swimming improves. I swim calmly and methodically along the riviera in the loveliest sound the world can offer. The current is rather weak here. I part the waves off my childhood shores stroke upon stroke as when I was young. For a moment I relive a few lines from Evert Taube's The letter from Lillan: "The water is warm and I swim every day and since I'm a good swimmer, I jump in right away."

"I'm a good swimmer." The refrain stays with me as I swim past Fria Bad and Pålsjöbaden. At Vikingstrand I get out. Though people who don't think summer is the best time to swim probably have never walked after swimming along the shore of the loveliest summer city in the Nordic region, I intend to walk back along the beach.

'Polar bear' Paradise

Some people swim during the summer, but many have gathered that you can jump in at any time. Winter swimming is a strong tradition in Helsingborg and I began while I was still a teenager. They were short, cold dips after long séances with old fogies who have been in the sauna long enough for their hair to fall out and their stomachs grow to football size. There was name-dropping and long stories with jokes so obvious the laughs preceded the punch line.

Pålsjöbaden in winter dress.

My venue has been between the harbour and Pålsjöbaden. The first years it was with my mother and my two sisters at Pålsjö. Then I moved to the cold baths called Kallis – perfect for small boy who could almost hide behind the rocks and spy on the naked women who used stairs to go into and out of the water. As a teenager it was Fria Bad. During my summer jobs in the harbour

Only
Hearts
M 044
dihelsingborg.se

The lovely coast continues northwards past Fria Bad towards Sofiero, Laröd, Hittarp and Domsten.

at a time when there were still stevedores there, we swam from the Järnvägmännens quay. Named after the railway workers, it harks back to the time when the huge greensward at Gröningen was a shunting yard. The workers only needed to cross the rails and jump in at the quay – swim suits were unnecessary. You can still swim nude in the area – all you have to do is climb over the wall and drop your clothes among the rocks.

So when is the city at its best? Those who have lived by the Sound for many years know that every season has its own charm. The oldest can tell of war winters with skating and hot-dog sales on a frozen Sound. Still, in spite of icy winters, autumn storms and spring months when rain clouds park between Kronborg and Kärnan, there is no European city where the feel of summer is as strong. Naturally the most important reason is the location, but while travellers in the 1900s complained of poor usage, today's can enjoy constant improvements.

Rejuvenated shoreline

A vital transformation came when the railway moved underground. This event has rejuvenated the entire northern shoreline. Many of the old harbour buildings were levelled and the quay filled with museums and flats. The bridge in Norra Hamnen has created a lively boating scene and moved Parapeten to within walking distance to downtown. When the city planners created a palm beach along the Parapeten wall, journalists from all over the country took the road to Helsingborg wanting to know if it really was as great as the rumours said. It is! Tropical Beach is a wondrous start on the long riviera.

For the new to come, the old must go – there is only so much sea to go around. As I wander along the water in Helsingborg I would personally want more of the old to give way. I would prefer to level the petrol station at Margaretaplatsen and replace it with a real skyscraper with a large garage under the shore ridge at the park.

Tropical Beach – an exotic beach downtown.

The summer 2007 the city not only provided a wooden sun deck and quays outside Gröningen, but the path along the Sound has become wide and grand. Now the walk north as far as Pålsjöbaden satisfies all requirements for a real riviera. The result is surprising for the residents have not applauded the new until it has become a bit older. By then the

The ferries cross the Sound every 20 minutes come rain or shine, storm or calm weather.

opposition to the new has turned into a feeling that it actually is better than they had thought. The truth is that many residents cannot imagine anything new that is not like the old. Helsingborgians are a conservative group; nothing can be demolished without protests. It is striking that the largest demonstration in city history was to preserve the old theatre. When the new library was planned for the city park during the 60s, the protests turned into riots and stone throwing. And when the new museum was planned in Norra Hamnen thousands signed protest lists saying it should be somewhere else. Nor was taking down the silos popular. The list of protests against the modernisation of Helsingborg is as long as the Sound. It is admirable that the city leaders have had the courage to resist.

Where in the city does one get the best feel of the sea? Everywhere is the simple answer to the hard questions. A deeper answer calls for more words. Personally I like variation, something many miss when they head for the same beach like pre-programmed robots. To discover all the special places along the coast calls for a restlessness.

If that restlessness is as strong as mine, a good condition follows. I was twenty when I first left Helsingborg to see the world. Around midsummer I checked with the long distance lorry drivers at the ferry terminal. The first hop took me to Basel. I continued round Europe during the late summer and autumn, returning in time for Christmas. Since then I have left many times and returned with impressions from all round the globe. The trips have changed my view of my hometown.

The sea is always there

Each time I return, my appreciation of what meets me has grown. When far away in a foreign city I stand and look out over the sea, I often think that it is almost as lovely as in Helsingborg. Few cities are as intimate with the water.

San Francisco and Istanbul are and Venice certainly – after all, it lies in the sea. This may sound like indiscriminate admiration for my childhood city, and would be if I stopped here. But I don't, for even if I like what I see as I perambulate round Helsingborg, I miss what has not yet been implemented. The pearl can yet have more lustre.

City planners, builders, restaurateurs and many others have made success of the beaches by the harbour. For the sections to the north to be as good, solid solutions are needed; sometimes radical ones. The Pålsjöbaden entrance must be moved closer to the Sound, perhaps with a terrace all the way to the water. In that way a large open place is won where Drottninggatan, Strandvägen and the road from Pålsjö Woods meet, with proper paths for cyclists and pedestrians.

The pilots' house on the parapet was first lit on October 24, 1889.

It is not by chance that the stories about the sea and Helsingborg play to the north. Southwards the city still awaits its meeting with the Sound. A tunnel to move trains and cars underground will be built. Only then can streets and buildings be built near the water, reshaping the old avenue between the city squares into a normal city street. A magnificent skyscraper at the tip of quay where the Oslo ferries once docked could make Turning Torso seem like an ordinary apartment house.

But whatever, when the house-owners in Rydebäck and Hittarp grow too old to care for their gardens and Campus Helsingborg recruits students from near and far, it is still the Sound that is the magnet. It cannot be much lovelier than it is in Helsingborg.

Following page:
Tropical Beach from above.

The Helsingborg Brand

By Bengt Håkansson
Branding expert, author and lecturer

I wonder whether there are any who are as proud of their city as Helsingborgians are. In all my years here I can't remember meeting anyone with a negative attitude. Of course there are opinions about both this and that, but on the whole nothing seems to change the idea people have that they live in the best of all cities. The same is true when you meet natives in exile – they may feel OK about where they are and have no plans to move back, but they still have a special warmth in their voice when they start to talk about their Helsingborg.

Naturally Helsingborg is not alone in having its local patriots. Still, you can easily get the idea that Helsingborgian pride sometimes goes a bit beyond normal bounds. An old book from 1955 tells us how it is: there are three types of Helsingborgians. The first type are the "real" natives, those who were born here and live here too. The second were also born here, but live somewhere else. And finally the third are those who live here right now, but who were born somewhere else. On that scale I, as born in Östergötland, understand that I will never climb higher in the pecking order, but must be resigned to be at least one class below my own, locally born children.

Now a love that is so strong and so eloquently expressed naturally carries with it equally strong and expressed ideas about how the city should develop. Not to mention how it should be marketed to the out-

Previous page:
Sunset in Kattegat. Helsingborgians feel that nearness to the sea is the most important ingredient for a great city.

The harbour and ferries in central Helsingborg – the city and the water in constant interplay.

side world. The question of what ought to be the city's profile or brand has been thrashed about forever, by both the city leaders and the man on the street. Today the question is hotter than ever, what with an increasing awareness of the importance a clear message outward in order to attract companies, available labour, tourists and other visitors.

It was against this background that we decided in 2005 to join up with the local powers that be and, putting aside both old and new ideas about the brand Helsingborg, begin to find out how the city is actually viewed. Nine hundred years old, Helsingborg cannot have avoided leaving impressions both nearby and far afield; changing people's fixed ideas is among the most difficult thing to attempt. Far better is finding out what pictures already exist and hopefully use that information as a foundation.

Our study included three external target groups. The first was a nationally representative sample of private individuals; the second a number of decision-makers in the Swedish business community within the for us especially interesting transport and logistics segments; and the third a choice group of journalists in both printed and broadcast media, all important opinion leaders. In this way we hoped to find out if the Helsingborgian pride had any support outside the city limits or if it only was an expression of local patriotism.

Naturally we took the chance to let the locals talk as well, in part to hopefully get down in writing that they actually liked and are proud of their city and also to try to understand what their positive attitude in fact comes from. So we included a group of individuals who had lived in Helsingborg for at least five years, as well as a group of corporate leaders in local companies with at least 20 employees.

Everyone was asked to answer the same questions, aiming at finding out if private persons had a different picture of Helsingborg than say a higher manager in a transportation company.

How many can consider living and working in Helsingborg?

In the first part of the survey, the respondents were asked to say which cities they would consider living and working in if they had a free choice. Among ordinary Swedes the top three were as follows:

Göteborg	60 %
Stockholm	48 %
Helsingborg	**40 %**
Halmstad	39 %
Lund	33 %
Malmö	32 %
Linköping	29 %
Umeå	26 %
Karlskrona	25 %
Jönköping	24 %

In other words, Helsingborg was an honourable third. Malmö actually came no higher than sixth place. Naturally it is interesting to find out what the 60% who did not choose Helsingborg think about our city. The answer is that most of them have no opinion at all, a rather positive position actually since it is always easier to build up new perceptions than to change old, deeply held ones.

The group of top managers in Swedish transport and logistics companies thought even better of Helsingborg:

Göteborg	50 %
Helsingborg	**46 %**
Halmstad	42 %
Malmö	38 %
Stockholm	34 %
Jönköping	27 %
Umeå	25 %
Lund	25 %
Linköping	20 %
Karlskrona	9 %

Here Helsingborg climbed up a notch. Note that though Göteborg remained on top, its position was weaker with this group than with ordinary Swedes. The same is true of Stockholm – the capital dropped to fifth place.

Best marks, however, came from the journalists – six of ten could imagine themselves working here:

Göteborg	72 %
Helsingborg	**62 %**
Stockholm	56 %
Halmstad	54 %
Malmö	52 %
Linköping	40 %
Lund	40 %
Umeå	34 %
Jönköping	30 %
Karlskrona	24 %

Without looking too closely at the exact percentages, we can still say that Helsingborg is one of the cities with the best reputation. In other words, there is cause for Helsingborgians to be proud of their city! At the same time there is much still to be done in the marketing area.

Ordinary Swedes said that 80% of them had visited Helsingborg, though only around half of them had managed to form an opinion of the city. This suggests that many only passed through going somewhere else. In other words, it's not enough to get people to come – we must be able to provide them with attractive, memorable experiences once we have them here.

What do people want from an attractive city?

In the second section of the survey we looked deeper. First we asked for the characteristics of an attractive city, that is how the ideal city would look if the person could choose. Then we tried to find out the degree to which the different cities manage to live up to that ideal.

Ordinary Swedes pointed to seven characteristics that most of them thought especially important, if they were free to choose a city to live and work in:

1. Naturally lovely surroundings 94 %
2. A city with safety and security 91 %
3. Top community care services 89 %
4. Excellent communications 87 %
5. Good access to open-air activities 86 %
6. Living, attractive downtown area 80 %
7. Closeness to ocean or water 80 %

You have to agree that on most points this list seems almost custom-made for a city like Helsingborg. And even better, the list is almost identical to the one the top managers and journalists drew up.

The blocks around Norra Hamnen are part of making central Helsingborg attractive.

Seashore in Viken, one of many popular residential places outside Helsingborg. Kullaberg Mountain can be seen in the background (188 m).

Which city is closest to the ideal?

Reality is one thing – perceptions of reality quite another. As it turns out neither Helsingborg nor any other city comes even close to matching the ideal. The explanation isn't that anyone has another conception, but rather that so many have none at all. Even when it comes to the country's capital the conceptions are vague to say the least. Less than half of those asked think that Stockholm does not "have many sights and attractions", nor "an excellent cultural selection." It seems that every Swedish municipality has a huge job ahead when it comes to selling oneself to those who live here.

All the more important then to look at what those who actually have a conception think. When it comes to Helsingborg, the seven strongest, most obvious characteristics are these:

1. Closeness to ocean or water
2. Attractive for tourists and visitors
3. Naturally lovely surroundings
4. Good access to open-air activities
5. Excellent selection of restaurants
6. Excellent communications
7. Living, attractive downtown area

It seems that Helsingborg's profile lies rather close to that of the ideal city for all three target groups. The only problem is that so many have yet to have an opportunity to form a conception of the city and to discover it superb characteristics. (A bit over 60% don't even know that Helsingborg lies close to an ocean or water!) Yet point five on the list should serve as an inspiration, for it's fantastic that Helsingborg has managed to build a reputation of note for its restaurant culture in a relatively short time.

So what do the Helsingborgians think?

As is usually the case, the best is saved for last.

Nearly all Helsingborgians asked, including both private individuals and top managers, agree that Helsingborg is an excellent city to live and work in. Indeed, just over 80% think it is better than any other city in Sweden!

The Helsingborg Symphony Orchestra gets high marks in both Sweden and abroad.

It would be interesting to know if the Helsingborgians are some special type of people, with other preferences and opinions than ordinary Swedes overall.

When it comes to the requirements for the ideal city, there are actually two points that the locals place higher than all the others. Again, for both individuals and top managers we're talking about:

1. Closeness to ocean or water
2. Excellent cultural selection

Private individuals added three additional characteristics, indicating that Helsingborgians not only look for personal comfort, but also want to live in a city that is so interesting and representative that it can be shown to others with pride:

1. Attractive for tourists and visitors
2. Handsome architecture
3. Lots of sights and attractions

Naturally the last and obvious question is if the picky Helsingborgian thinks the city lives up these high expectations. And the answer is an unreserved yes – on nearly every point Helsingborg fulfils the expectations of the residents completely. In several areas the expectations are exceeded by a good margin, especially among the municipality's city leadership.

Helsingborg boasts the oldest city theatre in the country. Here are Maria Kulle, Louise Ryme and Tobias Borvin in the musical Cabaret.

Sweden's smallest metropolis

It is an old rule of thumb that when it comes to building a brand, you should always take good care of the success factors you already own. Or put another way:

If you know why your current customers buy, you also know how to recruit new ones.

In the case of Helsingborg this means that we should start with what those who already love the city above all other cities think and convey their picture to all those who have yet to get to know us. When it comes to requirements on a residential town, the Helsingborgians are no different than most Swedes, if we ignore the fact that they have somewhat higher demands. In other words, there should be many potential Helsingborgians among those who just don't know it yet.

So let us finish by seeing what everyone who favours Helsingborg over all other cities think about their city, regardless of whether they are private individuals, top managers or journalists and regardless of whether they live in Helsingborg right now or not. The following eleven (!) characteristics were indicated as typical by at least eight of every ten in this group:

The bridge Kvickbron in Norra Hamnen.

Closeness to ocean or water	100 %
Naturally lovely surroundings	94 %
Attractive for tourists and visitors	93 %
Excellent communications	91 %
Good access to open-air activities	87 %
Excellent selection of restaurants	86 %
Living, attractive downtown area	85 %
Excellent cultural selection	81 %
Excellent selection of entertainment	81 %
Lots of sights and attractions	80 %
Good shopping city	80 %

There is much here to communicate, though after thinking about it, maybe it all combines to just one theme:

The city that offers most of the atmosphere and possibilities of a metropolis, but is spared many of the disadvantages thereof. A large city yes, but small enough to be tangible and possible.

Following page:
Recently Helsingborg has gained a reputation of being a first-class restaurant city, in much thanks to such TV-stars as Tina Nordström and Niklas Ekstedt, not to mention top-ranked eateries such as Gastro and Sofiero Slottsrestaurang.

Helsingborg on film

By Maja Ljung
Journalist and writer

If I close my eyes and think 'culture', 'film', 'Helsingborg', I can see my father's boyhood friends in the city of the 50s'.

Each time I round this curve on the road from Viken towards northern Helsingborg I hear his soft voice, bubbling with impish laughter, telling me about how his all-too-young mate pinched a car, slid off the road and flipped it.

As the copper neared, that the car radio was still blaring, there in the middle of the field, shamed him most. So he climbed in and turned it off.

That story and many more about my father's Helsingborg are my inner film. Or rather, a film intro to my life. Through the stories of the city I visited often as a child, I developed a view that the city was vital, a scene that shaped us and that we later never really leave. The city becomes a never-ceasing wellspring of events – of dangerous, fantastic, moulding events.

My city became another. This Skåne child moved to the university city Lund, fell in love and formed a family. Children grow up and look back. Some make films, but not me. But I still can't drop the thought that more than anything else film is a fantastic medium for exploring

Previous page:
Summer sees the start of bicycle tours. The film *Hata Göteborg* is about football hooligans, love and daring, such as cycling through all of Helsingborg.

what it is to be adult. Or to be really young. Making film is trying to recreate something of the intense flow of time from childhood and youth, of days and minutes. To find some structure for one's inner pictures.

Investing in youth

There is a film wonder aborning in Helsingborg. Its been called Hollyborg and young film is pushed hard. Louise Leghammar is film teacher at Film Helsingborg and works out of the Dunkers Cultural Centre. The city's Cultural Amenities Department asked her to draw youth to Helsingborg to make film, to support and inspire them regardless of film type or genre.

"Film Helsingborg is to be a hothouse, a proving ground. The films made will not be vetted. That's not my job."

Some of her plans are nearing fruition. Work has begun with the city library and the youth section Cinematica at the city's Filmstudio. A tour round the city's youth centres is planned, aimed at getting those young people who are dreaming film to dare. If only for a minute. Louise helps them write script, record, edit and clip.

"Telling your story is what matters. But film is a new medium and they need help making their own films."

Being young means searching. Maybe young Helsingborgians have no film interest at all. Louise is a realist.

"Maybe they all want to play in a band – the whole bunch. What's important is that I give them the tool for telling their own story. Then they can make their own choices. Film-making is both cheaper and easier today."

Regional actors

Helsingborg politicians believe in regional film, especially filmed in the city, by and with Helsingborgians. They have invested three million kronor in a media centre for filmmakers somewhere between amateur and professional. Another decision is to earmark another million annually to work with Film in Skåne promoting filmmakers under thirty.

Film in Skåne's youth film advisor Lotta Andgren is at the Dunker Cultural Centre several days each week. She hands me a flyer:

"You've heard about Pixel?"

This ten-year old short-film festival serves as a carrot for young filmmakers. You are visible when you show films outside the family. Being a teenager and seen. And getting a little help telling your story. That's what it boils down to.

But telling stories on film costs. Money and films are linked. A big film can create work, as well as pulling both money and fame to the city. Just look at Ystad Studios that a few years after the launch is up to speed making films where dolled-up local politicians ate superb food and dreamt Wallander and Beck dreams. Tourists abound. Film is glamour. We're all seduced.

"The politicians hope for a big film here too, one that'll provide work and more. But first you have to set the stage," explains Louise Leghammar.

A city stage: being a part of the kerbs, of remarkable public decorations and stone-faced hierarchies. A check on Helsingborg's website gives me info on the "security walks" city civil servants go on with the citizens since 2003. They wander through various districts to see things that can feel unsafe. "We're talking about poor lighting, too much greenery or more activities for district youths."

The new wooden deck at Gröningen is nearly unmarked. Öresund Sound is old and the light is fantastic. The deck seems to be accepted as a new resting space in the city, as well as a stage and a passage.

Growing up

Being young is painful. Being young and waiting for life is like stepping on egg shells, like flying and crashing, and then, hopefully, becoming strong. The successful director Robert Lillhonga points to Gröningen's new wooden decks:

"On the old deck the workers sat on one side and the well-to-do on the other. It 's true!"

Today groups of young people spread out side by side on the soft planks. Some restless souls kick a ball, others oogle the girls and rub on suntan oil.

"I met an old mate the other day. He said he hadn't been in the Söder district since he was twenty. Seven years ago!"

Robert's long-film debut Hata Göteborg (Hate Gothenburg) got mostly great reviews – a low-budget film with young hearts on offer and an unfailing touch to the dialogue. The film deals with gang roles;

Director Robert Lillhonga simply let the actors socialize as much as they could through a whole summer. Without manuscript, but within their respective roles. The result was the full-length film *Hata Göteborg*.

with the fear of being the mobbed, the outsider. Fear can push a person to most anything, such as beating up a football huligan or following a despotic gang leader.

"Gang roles are fixed in the lower schools. Where you grow up plays a vital role. The film's Mittander and Lukas could have been something very different. No one is good or evil – everyone is everything. My message is to dare to keep up, to take the step," exclaims Robert and immediately lowers his voice. The sidewalk café is full of lunchers and Norra Hamnen of rakish sail boats.

When he was ten he moved from a villa in Hjärup to a flat in Drottninghög and then to Fredriksdal. He talks about the city as if there were an invisible, razor-sharp line through it dividing north from south. He calls it sick that young people can live so differently in the same city and in the next breath he states that everyone must find the strength to shape, to change his or her own life.

"It is a philosophical dilemma," according to Robert Lillhonga.

Worlds meet

In the film a new world opens up for the gang from Söder when a cousin from Göteborg pops up, a guy in their age, but a traveller who is open to other people. In no time, the cousin gets to know Helsingborgians – from north. Shortly thereafter we see parts of the gang on a bicycle trip to Mölle northwards up the coast. "Cycling with cool chicks – Mittander should see us now," says the lead character and gang coward, a Fredriksdal resident. A new world opens up beyond north and south, beyond the hard gang hierarchy and hate-fed comradeship.

The rap music in *Hata Göteborg*; jazz and dance band in the 1976 film classic *Sven Klangs Kvintett* directed by Helsingborgian Stellan Olsson.

In his upper teens Robert cycled from Drottninghög and Fredriksdal to Mölle. He drank in the beauty and of the thought that no one owned the right to that tour more than anyone else.

"It's not natural for everyone to think that way," he says.

The actors gave a summer to the filming. In their role figures they went to the recreation centre on the steam ferry and played billiards and they rode the ferry without getting off, drinking beer. Over time the story took shape and the scenes took form.

Robert laughs and fills his glass with Ramlösa.

"That's how it was to film – impossible. But it's damn great that it worked. Now I think I can do everything."

It's the collective he likes. Creating large happenings with lots of people in front of and behind the camera, in an atmosphere lacking prestige where you try to avoid all internal jealousies. He started towards the late 90s with "three awful plays" at the Gyllene Prag restaurant in Helsingborg and continued with Gummitarzan (Rubber Tarzan) for adults and a play about the Roskilde Festival at Tivoli – the last with lots of people behind and up front and music from the Helsingborg group The Sounds. The Roskilde play grew and at the end played to standing room only in a circus tent on the Roskilde Festival campground. It closed with a shout in 2000, the same year the Pearl Jams gig at Roskilde ended with chaos and nine deaths.

Today the old steam ferry terminal is the city's rock stage.

The music for Robert Lillhonga's film on the Roskilde Festival is by the Sounds with vocalist Maja Ivarsson.

It seems so simple – Lillhonga wanted to do things for youth, about youth. Wanted to reach them where they live and bleed. Nor was he alone then in the early 2000s. The group started to call itself Theatre Incompetent, the second word because they lacked training and the "right stage-school accent". They put on several plays and made short films. At the same time as Robert began filming Hata Göteborg, he started to document the work at the Stumpenteater in Helsingborg, working with the homeless and mentally ill, with junkies and alcoholics.

"Helsingborg is very segregated, creating lots of anger, but is also inspiring, a way to exist in both worlds. This can give you the strength to do something. My motor has always been to show that we don't have to be enemies."

So where are the ladies?

Robert Lillhonga pedalled to Mölle from Drottninghög and Fredriksdal. My father, son of Tågaborg, took his wheels down a "rather good, freshly paved downhill in the middle of the delightful Pålsjö Woods", letting the whistling wind fill him with life. That's another of his stories.

A bicycle means freedom. Two-wheeling through the city you cross your own tracks, peek in where other people live and maybe find new paths. You grow up, loose friends, win others. The gang explodes, bleeds, disintegrates to make space for maturity. Another gang grows, becomes creative, shapes plays, music and films.

My father's stories, Roberts' and stories about stories. But where are the ladies? Forty percent of the large group working on the play about

Roskilde were girls. A year later, the percent stood at ten. What happened? Where are the mother stories? The girls' stories? Are they secret? Have the urban bushes grown so thick that the city can no longer be an amazing place for everyone?

Film pedagogues stand in line to explain why so few films are made by women. The answers are usually that the film world is conservative, filled with old fogeys; that girls don't stay the course, don't have the energy, do other things.

We'll see. The long film Fjorton suger (Fourteen sucks) was filmed in Helsingborg, released in 2005 and is told by a fourteen-year old girl. Louise Leghammar tells us girls are contacting her to make films.

Maybe we'll soon hear those mothers' stories filmed through their daughters' lenses. May one of those stories will be the hit film the politicians are hoping for. So watch out, Helsingborg!

Following page:
The road through Pålsjö Wood.

No return for Magnus Stenbock

By Anders Donelius
Writer and editor

What is so unusual about Helsingborg? Is it the location on Öresund Sound, the Danish proximity or the mighty Landborg shore ridge that lends the city an unmistakable character? Then again it might be the foghorns in November or the fact that it rains from the side and not from the sky as in the rest of the country? Whatever it is, there are things that have marked the city throughout history and still shape conceptions of Sundets Pärla – the Pearl of the Sound. This short course is designed to make things easier for you when talking with Helsingborgians.

City Hall

No, you're not in Venice. While it's true that the sixty-five metre clock tower will take your thoughts to the campanile in the city of gondoliers, you are actually in Sweden. The Helsingborg City Hall was built 1892–96 and, quoting art historian Torkel Eriksson in his book on the edifice, is a "mighty expression of the spirit and taste of the city called the consul's Helsingborg". Architect Alfred Hellerström's neo-Gothic creation is a melange of German, Italian, Dutch and English Gothic styles. Over the years the immense building with its old-fashioned, pompous architecture was much criticised, but today there are few who can imagine the Helsingborg cityscape without it. In fact, it's become almost as natural a part as Kärnan.

Previous page:
City Hall with its sixty-five metre clock tower is reminiscent of the famous campanile in Venice.

The grand Terrace Stairs lead from Stortorget up to Kärnan. They were built on initiative of Consul Oscar Trapp and inaugurated in 1903 by another Oscar, King Oscar II.

Kärnan

No building is as Helsingborgian as Kärnan. The oldest parts of this medieval castle keep were built in 1313 as a royal residence in Helsingborg Castle, at that time a vital player in keeping Skåne and the rest of Denmark united. In the late Middle Ages the castle lost its purpose and after the Swedish conquest it was rebuilt as a gun turret, storehouse and jail. When the castle was demolished in the 1680s, the keep remained as a ruin to be saved for posterity by a renovation in 1893–94. In spite of its rather modest 35-metre height, the tower is majestic where it stands on the shore ridge above the Terrace Stairs, looking down over the Stortorget Square and out over the Sound.

The Magnus Stenbock Statue

The winners always write history, which is why the statue of Count Magnus Stenbock stands on Stortorget in Helsingborg. He was Governor General in Skåne and ordered to defend the province against the Danes. As victor at the battle of Helsingborg on February 28, 1710, he drowned the last Dano-Scanian hopes of reunion in blood. In Swedish history, Stenbock is the heroic liberator of Helsingborg, but there are those who see him as the tyrannical oppressor of a population still friendly with the Danes. However, all protests were in vain and there he sits with his gaze fixed on the western neighbour. Still as history is want to do, the Danes got their revenge – three years after that battle, Stenbock was captured and died a Danish prisoner in 1717.

Sculptor Johan Börjesson's statue of Magnus Stenbock from 1901 is probably the only equine statue in Sweden of a non-royal person.

The Maria Church

Towards the close of the 1100s a small sandstone Romanesque church was built on the beach below the shore ridge. When the city population grew in the 1300s, today's Maria Church was built and stood ready in 1410. It has a high nave and two

The Maria Church lies in the middle of a cemetery used until early 1800s. Today it is very much alive with a seething restaurant life that suggests games of a more secular nature.

side aisles and is built in Danish brick Gothic. Among the church furnishings are the 15th century altar screen, the silver collection in the sacristy basement and the memorial tablet over the famous composer Dieterich Buxtehude, organist here in the mid-1600s.

Ramlösa

In Sweden Ramlösa has become synonymous with mineral water. The Scanian district medical officer Johan Jacob Döbelius vetted the well more than three hundred years ago. He claimed that the iron-rich water could cure several ills, including scurvy, gout and dizziness. Taking the waters at Ramlösa became the thing to do during the 1800s and many Scanian noble families built their own house in the lovely park.

The bottled Ramlösa water has its own history. It is taken from a well discovered when drilling for coal. The water proved alkaline and carbonated, of as high quality as the water from the famous European springs. The first water factory was built in 1912 next to the bathing house in the spa park.

One final point: Ramlösa has a short 'a'. The name comes from *ramm*, meaning moist meadow and *lösa* meaning either field or slope.

Ramlösa was the most famous spa facility in Helsingborg and has received high international acclaim for its bottled well water.

Sweden's first open-air museum lies in the area around the 18th century Fredriksdal estate.

Fredriksdal

Right in the middle of Helsingborg, but a few blocks from city centre, lies a time and a countryside as it was before the tractor. This is Fredriksdal, the country's first open-air museum. The complex has grown from the 18th century estate of diving engineer Fredrik Wilhelm Cöster and opened to the public in 1923 having been donated to the city by Consul Oscar Trapp's widow Gisela. In addition to the manor with its historic parks and gardens, there are some 50 historic buildings and various Scanian landscape forms with meadows, pastures, threatened native breeds and wild plants. The only disturbing noise in this idyll might be the clanging city smithy in the city district from the 1800s or applause from Fredriksdal Theatre next door.

"Every summer someone faints from laughter," says Eva Rydberg who took over the Fredriksdal Theatre in 1994 when her idol Nils Poppe retired.

The Fredriksdal Theatre

The Fredriksdal Theatre is a place dedicated to much laughter. It was built in 1927 in the French manner with trimmed hornbeam and lime tree hedges. Until the mid-1960s it served as a summer theatre with actors from Helsingborg's city theatre. At that time the well-known comedian and actor Nils Poppe took over and his comedies turned it into a national attraction. The Poppe era came to an end in 1994 when he handed the baton to Eva Rydberg, another recognized comedian, who has taken the tradition of full houses every summer evening into the next century. Even when it rains.

Sofiero

HRH King Gustaf VI Adolf spent sixty-eight summers at his beloved Sofiero just north of Helsingborg. His grandfather King Oscar II had commissioned the pleasure palace in 1865 and forty years later he turned it over to Gustaf Adolf and his consort Margareta of Connaught as a wedding present. A niece of HRH Queen Victoria of Great Britain, the future Crown Princess turned the slumbering park into a true model garden. Though she died in 1920, Gustaf Adolf continued to develop the garden as she had planned and his impressive rhododendron collection still draws visitors from near and far. Many Helsingborgians remember to this day when the King's blue train car rolled into the city's railway station. It was a sure sign of summer.

When King Gustaf VI Adolf died in 1973, his will stated that Sofiero would be turned over to the city. The glorious flowers in the garden bring many thousand visitors each year.

A few years ago when a US sports giant tried to copy the classic tennis shoe from Helsingborg, the New York Times reacted: "Great, Tretorns are back! But wait, what's that Nike swosch doing on the side?"

Tretorn

Once upon a time the whole world wore rubber overshoes from Tretorn in Helsingborg. During much of the 1900s Henry Dunker's factory was by far the city's largest employer with many playful pet names. When people stopped using overshoes, the trademark shifted its fame to rubber boots, tennis balls and sports shoes. The white gym shoes from Helsingborg were much sought after on the other side of the Atlantic, with the Canvas Nylite model gaining such a legendary status at US colleges that it was given a place in the Official Preppy Handbook for 1980. Today Tretorn is owned by the international sports group Puma.

Trädgårdsgatan

The street Trädgårdsgatan was built in the 1870s and is one of the city's many well-preserved avenues with elegant façades and high-class architecture. What separates it from the other fashionable streets is its position as the boundary between the well-to-do northern part of town and the less affluent south. However, when the downtown district expands southwards during the coming decades, this boundary will probably be retired to the history books.

Trädgårdsgatan forms the boundary between north and south in Helsingborg.

Helsingborg IF

Few Swedish cities support a football team as Helsingborg does. This does not mean that all Helsingborgians like HIF, but everyone has opinions about the team and demand that the team wins every game. But even that is not enough. "In this city it's not enough to win. You must win with panache," opined an earlier trainer.

The Helsingborg Sports Association (HIF) was formed in 1907 and is seen as one of the country's classic teams. It was at its height between the wars when it dominated the league and won the top division four times between 1928 and 1934. Yet another gold was taken in 1941, but a sixth title didn't come until 1999. The following year the team qualified for the Champions League by beating Inter twice in decisive games.

The club's two most famous players are the legendary goalkeeper Kalle Svensson and the world-class forward Henrik Larsson.

In the 2000 season, HIF qualified to the Champions League by beating the Italian top-team Inter twice in decisive games. The winning goal was made by Michael Hansson at Olympia, much to the joy of his teammates.

After a merger with Nordvästra Skånes Tidningar 2001, HD is published in three editions: Helsingborgs Dagblad, Nordvästra Skånes Tidningar and Landskrona Posten.

Helsingborgs Dagblad

When a Helsingborgian talks about HD, it is seldom the Swedish High Court (Högsta Domstolen) or some motorcycle they mean. Here HD means Helsingborgs Dagblad. This daily was founded in 1867 and is the largest outside Stockholm, Göteborg and Malmö. Ove Sommelius was its Editor-in-Chief between 1924–1974 and the Sommelius family is still active in its development. One interesting fact is that HD bought the Helsingborg-Posten in the 1950s, a paper that once hosted such luminaries as authors Birger Sjöberg and Elin Wägner on its editorial staff – proof that there are literary models for today's journalists.

Pålsjöbaden

In Helsingborg summer is not the only swimming season. In the 1800s the city had several handsome open-air baths, all of which are gone, the victims of storms, fires or decay. All except one, that is. The Follin family built the first bathhouse at Pålsjöbaden in 1880. When the city bought the property in 1908, the "Follin bath-house" was rebuilt by architect Ola Anderson. The Pålsjöbaden is considered a unique facility in Sweden and is listed as culturally valuable.

Together the Råå and Norra open-air baths and Pålsjöbaden offer Helsingborgians an opportunity to take a sauna all year.

Råå Hamlet

In southern Helsingborg where the Råå Creek empties into the sea lies the Råå Hamlet. There have long been settlements here, but it was first

in the 1600s that they became permanent. Råå has been attacked several times and during the wars between the Danes and Swedes, the former landed here both June 29, 1676, and September 12, 1709. However, the worst invasion came on August 10, 1788, when the whole village was burned by a Russian naval squadron. The hamlet rose again and around 1900 Råå was one of the largest Swedish fishing hamlets with some three hundred fishers and 130 boats. Today it is an idyllic city district – houses facing the street, superb beaches and an impressive marina. It is important to remember that you live on Råå, not in. The natives are very sensitive on that point.

Helsingborg has nearly 20 km beach from Fortuna in the south to Domsten in the north. Fria Bad is one of the beaches right downtown.

Fria Bad

Fria Bad is the closest you can come to Copacabana without leaving Sweden. The site received official standing 1924 and though today's bureaucrats call it Örestrandsbadet, everyone else says Fria Bad. The beach consists of white sand that gives way to beach vegetation and grass further in. In the morning it is mostly older persons who come on foot in their bathrobes from their homes nearby. Daytime it is families with children and then young people take over the beach. After a cooling dip, the draw is the old ladies changing rooms, today a restaurant. Here you can enjoy a nice dinner and view the sun disappear into Kattegatt.

Kullagatan

Should you wish to locate the true centre of Helsingborg, it is probably the point where Stortorget Square meets Kullagatan Street. This is the favourite position for everyone who wants to get noticed, be it politicians or clowns. Once part of the original, medieval street system, Kullagatan became Sweden's first pedestrian street in 1961 and has been the main beat for Helsingborgians since. The street is full of shops and restaurants from Stortorget in the south to St. Jörgens Square up north. Earlier the name often used was Kullagågata, perhaps to emphasize the sensational in a street without cars.

Kullagatan became the country's first pedestrian street in 1961.

Olympia

A couple of years ago Olympia was named Sweden's finest football (soccer) stadium, but originally football was not on the agenda. It was cycling and skating that was discussed when industrialist and politician Malte Sommelius called a meeting in November 1895 to discuss the need for an arena. With Scanian winters being what they are, it was probably just as well that the ice skating rink wasn't built, but the cycling track was ready in May 1898 and the infield was prepared for football and track and field. The company that built the stadium was called AB Olympia and that is what the venue was called. With the successes of Helsingborgs IF, football took over and since 1985 the stadium is entirely given over to that sport. Even the city district to the west of the stadium is called Olympia and is known for its Art Nouveau architecture.

Olympia from 1898 has been rebuilt several times and is one of the country's classic football pitches.

Pålsjö Woods has long inspired romantic authors. But in Hans Alfredson's novel The Pålsjö Woods' Assassination terrible things happen in the ravines.

Helsingborg's expansion during industrialism stands alone in Sweden. The pioneers during that era were consuls, from left, Nils Persson, Oscar Trapp and Petter Olsson

The Consuls

In the latter half of the 1800s Helsingborg was "the city of consuls". Two of the leading were Petter Olsson (1830–1911) and Nils Persson (1836–1916). They became pioneers for the growing entrepreneurial spirit and led the city's transformation from a sleepy small town to a dynamic trade and industry city. Olsson and Persson started a large number of companies, worked together on municipal questions and both became members of the Swedish parliament. But privately they were opposites. Olsson was deeply religious with little time for pleasures, while Persson has been called a bon vivant and aesthete. And though they were active in the same city at the same period, it is said they were never on visiting terms. The third leading consul was Oscar Trapp (1847–1916). He played a vital role in the city's railway expansion and made strong contributions to its cultural life.

Pålsjö Woods

A green band runs through Helsingborg starting in the Råå Valley to the south. To the north lie the Pålsjö Woods, a popular promenade area for Helsingborgians. The woods are mostly filed with beech, but there are some oaks and alder as well. The area is quite varied, offering deep brook ravines, rare plants and lovely pastures. The edge of the shore ridge offers a singular view over the Sound and the Danish coastline. The woods have their name from Pålsjö Manor dating to the 1600s. Not far away is Thalassa, a magnificent patrician villa built around 1900 and currently serving as a youth hostel. The large promenade area stretches all the way to Sofiero to the north and beyond. The city's green band follows the shore ridge and the coast all the way to Domsten.

The city's first steamship for Sound traffic was launched in July 1856 and quite naturally named Helsingborg. Today there are three lines on 20-minute schedules.

"Tura"

To tura means riding the ferry back and forth between Helsingborg and Helsingör without getting off. The reason is to sit in one of the onboard restaurants and enjoy what's on offer. If you're having a really good time, you can double up or even do a triple. "Where are we?" is a frequent question on such a trip. In recent years this travelling has lessened, as the ferries have become more impersonal and the pub life in Helsingborg has grown, reaching continental proportions. But as Helsingborgians would say: "A turn around is always a turn around!"

Helsingör

It's only four kilometres to the city's western sister. Helsingör and Helsingborg have long lived as two city districts separated by a sound. As early as the 1400s the cities had a common market place – on one of the two weekly market days Helsingörians would come over to buy beef, pork, butter, cheese and eggs. Butchers and bakers from Helsingborg had shops on the other side. When Skåne became Swedish in the 1600s it was a natural divorce, but the feeling of being one unit straddling the narrow sound has remained. Today Helsingör is about half the size of its sister with a mixed commercial life and lively border commerce. The city is also a well-known tourist goal with the world-famous Renaissance castle Kronborg, Hamlet's Elsinore, as the main attraction.

Halsingar, later called hälsingar, were those who lived at the narrowest part of the Sound, the so-called Hals or neck. The sandy western coast was called Ören, while on the east lay the borg or castle; hence Helsingör and Helsingborg.

Henry Dunker

Helsingborg has many famous sons and daughters, among them Stellan Skarsgård, Hans Alfredson, Karl Ragnar Gierow and Sally Bauer. But none have meant as much to the city as industrialist Henry Dunker (1870–1962). He was the son of port engineer Johan Dunker who founded Helsingborgs Gummifabriks AB (Tretorn) with the support of the city's leader Consul Olsson. The son Henry took over in 1894 and became pioneer in Swedish industry. He built an international group, placing Helsingborg on the world map with his overshoes, rainwear, boots and tennis balls. Dunker was a hard man, but also took good care of the factory workers with free health care and subsidized medicine. He founded the corporate day-care centre Barnkrubban as early as 1911, one of the first of its kind. This shy industrialist gave his first interview on his 90th birthday, but it gave few answers that shed light on the private person Henry Dunker.

Henry Dunker became one of Sweden's richest persons. He willed his fortune to a foundation that is still a big shareholder in Trelleborg AB. Its grants have financed projects like the Helsingborg City Theatre, the new grandstand at Olympia Stadium, the Kulturmagasinet at Fredriksdal and the Dunker Cultural Centre.

Zoégas coffee

The recent "caffè latte trend" has taught Swedes that real coffee is dark-roast coffee. Helsingborgians have known that for more than a century. In November 1886 Carlos Zoéga started a small coffee roasting shop on Kullagatan 27. Of Italian stock, this merchant had run a coffee shop in Landskrona some years, but the natives there weren't really coffee enthusiasts. It was better in Helsingborg, though Carlos died as early as 1888 and his wife Maria had to take over. She married merchant Johan Svensson and their son Rudolf Zoéga was the one that piloted the company from handicraft to industry. Today Zoégas is owned by the international Nestlé Group and leads the Swedish market for dark-roast coffee.

The Zoégas store on Drottninggatan.

Jacob Hansen's House

The only burgher house in Helsingborg from the Danish period stands on the corner of Norra Strandgatan and Nedre Långvinkelgatan streets. Over the front door it says that Councillor Jacob Hansen and Inger Mogensdotter built the house in 1641. During King Karl XI's war in 1679 large sections of central Helsingborg were burned and destroyed, but the Hansen house survived and can still be seen today. It gives a good picture of the half-timbered houses that lined the city's main street in the 1600s.

The city's oldest residential house is now a popular meeting place where special events, company dances and lectures are held and enjoyed.

Norra Hamnen

Many a critical voice was raised when the plans to tear down the silos in the Norra Hamnen were presented. Today most agree that replacing them with housing was a successful transformation, so good in fact that the district has served as a model for the renovations in the old port sections of other cities. The area was inspired by Tegnestuen Vandkunsten in Copenhagen and was completed for the Housing Fair H99 in the summer of 1999. The architecture is modernistic and the houses are placed so that all flats enjoy a view of the Sound. It differs from the harbour projects in other cities in its central location, enabling it to become a living, vibrant city district.

Many visitors are fascinated by the Mediterranean feel in Norra Hamnen with its residences, shops, marina, restaurants and sidewalk cafes. Still on a windy January day, the sun feels far away.

The Helsingborg exhibition at Parapeten 1955 is remembered for two things: modernism's breakthrough in Sweden and the lovely summer weather.

H55

There rests a nostalgic shimmer over the summer of 1955. That was when Helsingborg arranged an international architecture and design exhibition that brought modernism's Swedish breakthrough. Many of the items shown left impressions that are still felt. For instance, the kitchen was presented for the first time as a functioning work site and Lena Larsson's newfangled idea of a living room came to stay. "Our tastes differ and our demands differ as well!" was the exhibition motto and it became the happy message of individualism and functionalism. It was also one of the bases for the Housing Fair H99 held at the same place almost 50 years later.

Concert Hall • City Theatre • Dunker Cultural Centre

Three Helsingborg cultural institutions form a golden triangle downtown. The City Theatre was built in 1976 and has two scenes, one large and the other small. Just fifty steps away is the Concert Hall where the Helsingborg Symphony Orchestra plays. The Concert Hall was built in 1932 and designed by Sven Markelius. It is seen as one of the foremost examples of Swedish functionalism. A few hundred

Today's City Theatre was finished 1976 and replaced the old theatre from the 1800s, torn down to violent protests from the general public.

The Concert Hall drew much attention for its modern architecture when it was inaugurated in November 1932.

After a discussion lasting 93 years on where the city museum should stand and over 200 architectural proposals, the Dunker Culture Centre in the Norra Hamnen was opened in 2002.

metres to the south stands the Dunker Cultural Centre, inaugurated 2002 with the proud ambition of "lifting Helsingborg into the world and the world into Helsingborg". The startling building was designed by Danish architect Kim Utzon, son of the world-famous Jörn Utzon who conceived the Sydney Opera House.

Landborgen

The mighty shore ridge ensures that Helsingborg differs from all other cities in the Öresund Region. The ridge or landborg is a raised plateau or more correctly, an abrasion cliff that stretches from the Ramlösa valley in the south to Domsten in the north. In part 40 metres high, it was formed when the land ice melted and through the millennia has been cut into deep ravines by waterways such as at Ramlösa, Pålsjö and Hittarp. Thanks to the shore ridge Helsingborg has many places with an impressive view over the Sound and many steep streets to bedevil the city's bicyclists.

The lovely nature of the shore ridge walk runs both north and south. From downtown you can choose to go north around six kilometres to Sofiero or south where you reach the Raus Church after eight kilometres. This is where Ruben Rausing rests, the merchant son from Råå who founded Tetra Pak.

If you want to know more about Helsingborg I can recommend Gösta Johannesson's book titled Helsingborg – City for 900 years (1980), and Helsingborgs stadslexikon (2006). There you'll find facts even a native doesn't know. For who knew that the spa Hälsan was run by a Dutch magician called Jacob Baladrega?

The footballer who came home

By Ken Olofsson
Journalist och TV-reporter

A rental car takes me in from the south, stopping a moment on the road to Olympia, a lump in my throat. Södergatan, the People's House, the bathhouse – places I knew as a child, in the Tempo House on the Gasverksgatan corner. At least that house still stands, as opposed to so many others, old buildings in this district, including the brewery by the fire station. That is where my Father worked and I in the summer as a bottle sorter. Cars and bicycles move towards the summer fields at Råå, but the trams are gone. I choose Nytorgsgatan and remember afternoon performances at the Roxy Cinema, today a religious house. Stop off at the grand neogothic Gustav Adolf Church from 1896-97 and drawn by Hermansson from Stockholm. I was confirmed there a long time ago. Outside is the square whose name was changed to Gustav Adolf's Square in 1909, but is still called Nya Torget by the people – flowers, fruit and vegetables are on offer and the language varies. This is a city district dominated by people of foreign extraction and the lowest average annual income of all Helsingborgians.

I remember the windy days that felt extra fiendish just there at Nya Torget. So did the poet:

Previous page:
Defender Erik Wahlstedt was recruited to HIF from IFK Göteborg in 1998. The next year he won the Swedish series with his new club.

Till döddagar skall jag väl minnas
hur det blåser i Helsingborg.
Till barken almarna skinnas
av vädret kring Nya torg.
Med järnspikar havsblåsten stinger
Stenbockens kopparbantlär
och rådhuset lyfter ett finger
att känna hur vinden är.

Until I die I will well remember
the winds in Helsingborg.
The elms are nearly dismembered
by the weather at Nya Torg.
The sea wind throws iron nails
at the copper artillerist
and City Hall checks in detail
just how windy it really is.

Karl Ragnar Gierow (1904–82), Permanent Secretary of the Swedish Academy 1964–77

Helsingborg became home

Football player Erik Wahlstedt came first to Helsingborg's northern district. Today the city is home to him and his family.

"This was in the 90s. I was playing in IFK Göteborg. We had an away game with Helsingborg and were on the bus to the game at Olympia. I remember the coffee fragrance from Zoéga and glimpsed Nils Poppe's Fredriksdal. That was all. You could guess that there was

Above:
Gustaf Adolf Square in the Söder district is called the GA-torget. The neo-Gothic church with the same name was built 1896-97.

much that was beautiful and good in this city. Now that I've moved here, I can't imagine living anywhere else. I'm here for good – there just can't be a better place to live your life."

But what does he think about the winters, the fog and the wind Gierow describes in his poem?

"No problem. You can always travel to sunny beaches when it's dark here. And if you like the west coast, you put up with the wind. It's part of it. I'm not particularly bothered by it since there are so many plusses. I can't say I've read Gierow and barely know who he was. I don't have time to read books, a hole in my life I'll have to fill later. But with four kids at home and football every week except a few around Christmas, I don't have time. Not yet."

Erik was born in April 1976 in Sollentuna north of Stockholm. But the family soon moved to Växjö where his father had found a job as local manager for the Linjeflyg airline. In 1986, they moved on to Halmstad. This is where Erik's football career got started. It was in BK Astrio that a fifteen-year old Erik first played as a forward paired with Mats Jingblad, member of the national team and Swedish champion in Halmstad BK. Today he is a successful coach at IFK Norrköping. Erik was discovered by IFK Göteborg and recruited in 1992. His first flat was in the Kallebäck district. He played ball and studied in a two-year social program. "But I had no idea what I would be. I had my eyes on a football career. Today, when I'm a bit older and wiser, I'm happy I didn't stop studying. It'll give me a base to stand on when my playing days are over."

Erik on the job. In the background is part of Olympia's east stands.

Big moments

Erik earned one of his two greatest football moments with IFK Göteborg. AC Milan was in town to play IFK in the Champions League on Ullevi, autumn 1996. With twenty minutes left, Erik was sent in. He crossed in front of the Milan goal as Niclas Alexandersson pushed the ball up on the right, passed world-famous Maldini and centred the ball. Erik ended up in header duel with Costacurta. "I took a half step back before the ball reached me. It was an odd touch, but it went in ..." The goal made it 1-1 and IFK Göteborg won by 2-1. The other big moment came on the gold night with HIF. He came to the Helsingborg club 1998, the same year they vied for the first gold since 1941 playing against a club already relegated. But it would be another year before they succeeded, on the same Ullevi pitch in Göteborg. The deciding gold match was against IFK Göteborg, Erik's old club.

"What I remember is the moment on the steps in front of Kärnan. Unbelievable!!! Raising the cup, listening to the screams, singing the club song and sharing the joy with all the great supporters. That rush is something I wish all athletes could feel. I'll never forget it: it was big and mighty and I try to think about that joy when the days are grey and down."

More lovely than Göteborg

Erik's first flat in Helsingborg was a bachelor's pad near Olympia. He got to know the city and its atmosphere and took special joy in the harbour, the Sound, Pålsjö Woods and the summer beaches.

"In some ways Helsingborg is a copy of Göteborg. Everything is near; the city feels intimate. But the shore ridge makes it lovelier. And the water is a part of the city's heart – it's always there when you're moving around downtown. I especially appreciate how close you are to all the baths. It only takes a few minutes to reach the beach from where you live. In Göteborg it's at least 10 kilometres or more. Getting there was a chore. Sun and swimming is important to my family and me during the summer half of the year. When we travel abroad, it's always for sun, never snow."

After the 2006 season, Erik was named HIF player of the year.

We meet him at work, at Olympia. The morning workout, the day's only one, is done. He's worried about some pain in a heel. "Maybe I'll miss the game on Sunday, but I don't want to." Erik is one of HIF's most experienced players and a backfield stalwart. He has played more than 200 matches in the top Swedish league, has 20 goals and two A-level international matches. He was chosen for the national team for the European Championships 2004.

Erik has played for Sweden twice so far, here in a match against Portugal 2004.

"That's the closest I've come to a really big series. I didn't play, but had a chance to feel the big game. Exciting!"

Return trip to Denmark

Erik was offered a contract with Esbjerg in Denmark for the 2001 season.

"Of course money was part of the decision. I got a chance to earn a sum I could invest for the future. And it was exciting to experience another country. The difference between living in Sweden and in Denmark is greater than you think. The Danes look at life and living differently. More relaxed. It's remarkable when we live so close to each other, but that's the way it is."

Erik also felt that the football was different.

"It's more open, more technical in Denmark. But better tactically in Sweden." It was now that Erik was shifted to the backfield. The trainer was Viggo Jensen, formerly at Malmö, who put him there in an emergency and he's been there ever since – a truly successful shift.

After three seasons in Esbjerg, Erik wanted back to Sweden. The choice was simple: back to Helsingborg. He had met his wife Cathrine, whose roots were deep in the Helsingborg soil. She had grown up in Eskilsminne and played well in division 2, representing

HDFF as libero. They have two children together, Izabelle at three and Elias at 1.5. Cathrine also has two children from a previous relationship, namely Robin 18 and Rebecca 15. Robin plays football in Helsingborg's Södra and Rebecca is close to a place on Eskilsminne's A-team. The family has always lived in Eskilsminne and just moved to a large bungalow in the same district.

Mommy Cathrine with Izabelle and daddy Erik with Elias outside the Eskilsminne villa.

"Helsingborg is the natural choice for me. Everything I appreciate is here. The city is just large enough and comes with charm, handsome settings and is good for children. It's close to Denmark and the continent. Then there are the many great HIF supporters. Football is tops in this city – a trip round the city or a shopping centre visit means many football talks. But I like that. Supporter involvement is fantastic!"

Five favourites

We ask Erik to name his five favourite Helsingborg places.

"Olympia, where I work: A charming, intimate, pitch. And the newly laid grass is wonderful. I'm one of those who think that football should be played on real grass!

Norra Hamnen: I like the architecture, the street life, the feel. Really well done!

Eskilsminne: A cosy district with an authentic small house setting. All of us have found roots. We're all very happy here. It's like a small city within the city – quiet, lovely, good neighbours, great solidarity. It's close to day care and schools, to downtown, to services. It couldn't be better!

Kärnan – a magnificent, mighty building. It's inspiring to stand up top and looking out over the harbour, the ferries and the Sound. It is a bit of Helsingborg's heart and soul.

Öresund: My father-in-law has a sailboat and we take short overnight trips with the children. Ven Island is a good goal. Our special places on the Danish side - Hornbæk, Gilleleje and Nivå are favourites!"

Future goals

His answer to a question about what he wants to achieve in his football career is quick and to the point:

"Another gold! I'd love to relive that long, lovely night in 1999. The club is so strong and the desire so great that if this is not the year, we'll do it before I have to stop. There is a football culture in Helsingborg. Almost everyone is involved, more or less. It's true that the greatest enthusiasts have the largest demands. Sometimes they don't understand that their team isn't up to snuff or doesn't win often enough. But the involvement is wonderful. Helsingborgians embrace both football and their HIF to the full!"

Erik wants to continue playing top-level football a bit longer. "As long as my health holds and I can contribute." But he knows the day will come when another life outside Olympia's gates takes over.

"Sometimes I wonder what I should be. Youth trainer maybe? Or gym teacher. Or something with economy. I'm not so sure right now. Life is so intense. Top-level football, family, wife and four kids, a new house… in fact, I only know one thing for sure: I'll never move out of Helsingborg!"

A taste of Lebanon

By Karin Liliedahl
Editor and reporter at the Helsingborgs Dagblad

First there were two types of snacks: chips and salted peanuts. Then came Hassan Sarris and now Helsingborgians fill up on his flavorous nuts. And he's right in there too, eating a fistful of the highest quality almonds each day. It's good for more than the stomach.

"They're truly nutritious. Zero cholesterol, since they're roasted," he says, leaning back in his desk chair in his office. His sanctum is a second story corner room at the Mixmaster company. From here he leads his nut imperium with pride – and with respect for the city he loves.

He started Mixmaster together with Magnus Hallin, previously CEO at Karamellkungen. The purpose was to package confectionery, but he had an ace up his sleeve. He wanted to show quality goods from his home country Lebanon by opening a luxurious shop called Tasty House to sell nuts, cakes and pastries.

Today Mixmaster has 110 employees; its subsidiary Tasty House has 120 and the nut roastery Nutisal another 50. The companies grow apace.

A new branch

When Hassan started Tasty House in the Söder district and later was part of setting up the nut roastery in the Väla Södra industrial park, it was a completely new industry that came to Helsingborg, just as when the Zoéga coffee roastery came to town. He linked up the city with the nut supplier Mohammed El Rifai, owner of larger roasteries in Lebanon and part owner of Nutisal.

Choosing Helsingborg felt completely right. The city had the conditions he needed to succeed with his company and for the family to be happy.

He came to Sweden and Stockholm in 1988 and started a small

Previous page:
A completely new industry has appeared in Helsingborg: The Nutisal nut roasting facility on Väla exports nuts all over Europe.

food and candy shop. Ever since childhood the family had told him he was a businessman. Even so he studied to be an architect at home in Lebanon, planning to build and sell houses as is still common in the Middle East. His parents had fled the problems in Israel, going to Lebanon. On his 23rd birthday a bomb filled his body with shrapnel and he spent several years in the hospital. So Hassan was also forced to

The Sarris family has settled in Husensjö. Bilal, Bassem, Samiha and Hassan at home in their villa.

flee together with his wife Samiha.

The shrapnel put an end to his favourite hobby. Now he has be happy just watching others play football; and of course HIF is his and his family's favourite team. He takes his VIP- season card from his desk drawer and pulls the tickets out like an accordion. His company is a gold-sponsor of the team.

"The whole family watches football," he says.

Lovely and close to the continent

The flight from Lebanon led to Stockholm, Kävlinge and Landskrona before landing at the goal: Helsingborg.

Mixmaster had moved here as early as 1996, the same year Hassan got to know Magnus Hallin. Mixmaster became their joint company. Today the company works with all large business chains, delivering smart, attractive packages filled with candy. Easter eggs is one of their bestsellers – three million of them are packed each year at Mixmaster in Helsingborg. They are sold all over the world through Ikea, though not here in Sweden. During the summer huge champagne bottles are filled with candy for Liseberg Amusement Park in Göteborg. He lists products galore that his company has developed.

The Sarris family followed the company to Helsingborg after a three-year house search. Then they had found their dream house in Husensjö. Hassan and Samiha settled there and it is there their three sons Khalid, Bassem and Bilal have gone to school.

"I liked the city from the first. It's lovely. On summer evenings we take a basket and go down to the beach. I walk along the water several times a week."

He looks out his office window and wonders where the sun is. The only thing he actually misses from Lebanon is just the sun – lately it's mostly rained.

This busy businessman travels often on business, almost always to Europe by car. That is another reason for establishing his company in Helsingborg – the continent is near. In short order he explains how quickly you get to Denmark, to the German metropolises and even further afield. He seems very satisfied.

Positive business culture

At the office Hassan Sarris offers standard fine-ground coffee in white mugs. But for a breakfast starter he usually takes a cup of Arabian coffee brewed with cardamom. The telephone on his desk rings continuously and he asks his secretary to take the calls while we talk. He works at creating a positive company culture, involving his employees.

"The feeling that we're building this together is important," he explains.

The Mixmaster subsidiary Tasty House is Hassan's baby. No one is surprised to see him there behind the counter at Tasty House on Södergatan. Suddenly he just stands there, stretches out a scoop of nuts and asks you to taste.

"I believe in my products and that's why I invite you to taste," he says.

Hassan Sarris likes to leave the office and stand behind the counter at Tasty House.

But on a closer look, it is also a question of a carefully thought-out business strategy.

"People are happy and positive when you offer a sample. Over eighty percent decide right after the sampler to buy nuts. And twenty percent tell someone else they were given a sample. It's the best advertisement we can get."

Just that sample costs the company more than a half million annually.

Knowledge from Lebanon

Hassan Sarris felt that there only were two kinds of snacks in Sweden, namely peanuts and chips. But Swedes travel a lot and have acquired a taste for more. He wants to teach them to eat nuts.

"The problem is that no one believed in my idea. Only me. It called for large investments. In Sweden you could only find the worst nuts. I wanted to show that something else existed and my friends who knew the market and I began to look for the products we sought."

It was then he first met Mohammed Al Rafai in Lebanon. And then the Tasty House concept was moulded, an elegant shop to sell nuts, nuts and more nuts in various taste combinations, as well as cookies from the Middle East and pastries. Bakers from Lebanon came up to Sweden and taught the personnel in the company's bakery how to get the right taste on baklava of every imaginable type. Helsingborgians learned quickly to like baklava – small cakes using filo pastry, almonds, honey and butter.

Hassan notes that Swedes are eager to both sample and buy, a rather important combination for the shop.

"It took two and a half years to find the right shop design, one that would display the best that Lebanon has to offer."

Today he feels that the Helsingborgians are best in Sweden on eating nuts.

"Once the younger set bought 400 grams candy for 30 kronor. Today they'd rather buy nuts, even though they only get 150 grams for the same money. That means a lot to me."

Expanding rapidly

Tasty House in the Söder district opened on September 26, 2005, though not without some stage fright on the part of both owners and new employees. They had gathered at Marina Plaza the evening before the doors would open.

"The staff asked me if I really thought we'd make it with our nuts, with the new concept. I knew it would work out."

By January 2007 fifteen nut shops have opened, in addition to shop-in-shop stores selling nuts, baklava and dried fruit as part of another store. The shops also have a café and ordinary candy for sale. Today Tasty House has gone international – in September 2007 a shop opened in Roskilde. At the same time the doors opened in Väsby outside Stockholm.

"We could easily build two-hundred shops in Sweden. But our organisation cannot keep up and it's hard to find the right shop sites." The shops look much the same. An architect office in Lebanon is responsible for the design and Lebanese carpenters come up and create complete shop interiors from the modules from Lebanon. Stepping into a Tasty House is like being transported to the most luxurious shops on the elegant streets in Beirut.

Thanks to their many trips abroad, Swedes have acquired a taste for nuts and dried fruits. The Tasty House shop concept is borrowed from Lebanon.

That the first shop was built in the Söder district of Helsingborg was mere chance according to Hassan Sarris.

"I hadn't thought about the fact that Helsingborg had a north and south. For me Söder was also Helsingborg and downtown at that. I have many customers from up north." He thinks that Söder will become a hot district when the city's plans for the area are realized.

The latest large step for Mixmaster is the Nutisal nut roastery in Väla Södra. Not only will it supply Swedes with nuts, but also export roasted, flavoured nuts to Europe. In time it will become one of the largest roasteries in Europe handling twenty thousand tons of nuts annually. When it became obvious that Mixmaster needed larger facilities for the roastery, as well as for the bakery, warehouse and administration, the company left the Berga industrial park and set up Väla Södra.

"The city helped us find the lot. Communications between us and those responsible was smooth and we worked out a deal that suited us," says Hassan and adds that it was quite clear that the city wanted the company to stay in Helsingborg when it was time to expand.

Following page:
Logistics, transport, food and media are prominent in the city's commercial life. In recent years a number of Swedish companies have chosen Helsingborg for their main offices, both for its geographic location and its excellent living environment. IKEA is one example. Its worldwide operations are currently controlled from the old sugar factory in the South Harbour.

Young People's City

By Christine Hansson
Freelance journalist and editor

Four teenagers from different parts of the city. Different worlds? Actually no! Marcus from Söder, Mathilda from Raus, Erik from Hittarp and Kelly from Dalhem have never met. But they agree on a lot – for example that in Helsingborg it's never far. To mates, practice halls or football pitches. To beach and abroad. Even to the city's own ski resort Våxtorp!

"As long as it's on Söder"

Marcus Toth steals out of a large, handsome street door where he lives with his mother – on Södergatan almost on Gustav Adolf's Square. The market is bubbling. The busy street life raises temperatures.

" It's great as long as it's on Söder," says Marcus brashly when asked where he wants to live. This is his block. His father lives a few blocks away towards Högaborg, comfortably close to Olympia when Marcus wants to play football.

"There are ten of us or so, mates who call each other during the week. Then we cut up to Olympia to kick a ball awhile. Mostly guys from my school, from Slottet."

Taking a break at Lindell's classic bakeshop, he says that the Slottsvångskolan where he's been for two years is tops.

"It's fun!" he says and starts to smile. "I went to a small school earlier, to Centrumskolan in Fredriksdal. It was a 0-9 school, but in the sixth it was too small. There were only five of us."

Life as a fifteen-year old is OK. His only worry, as he sees it, is Spanish – " it's all right." Then he says it as it is: "I'm definitely worst.

Marcus Toth, here in front of his school in central Helsingborg, lives in the Söder district, perhaps the area with the most potential in all of Helsingborg.

It was OK in the sixth, but since then it's downhill."

Instead Marcus' list of favourite subjects includes English, sports and math. The last with some reservation. "In other words, I don't like it, but Per-Olof, our teacher, is a scream!"

His best mate Mikael attends Wieselgrensskolan and they meet almost every day.

"We're not really alike. He doesn't really like football and I don't skate."

So they exercise in front of the TV using Nintendo Wii and Marcus explains by waving his arms.

"You're right there – what you actually do in front of the TV shows up on the screen."

Train using the TV. Parents of teenagers sense that the most powerful argument against TV-games, namely the poor health argument, has been pulled out of their hands. There's only one left: "You need fresh air!" OK. Let's open a window ...

And where is Marcus in a few years?

"It's not all there, but I think I want to be a chef or a bartender. But it's like this. You can't live on being a bartender when you're 40. Still, it'll probably be Hotel and Restaurant. If I don't change my mind."

The sun shines over the booths on GA Square. The wind catches the pants legs, making balloons on the hangers. They soon lift and kick about happily.

"I think I'll live here when I grow up," says Marcus philosophically, "or I'll move further out. It would be cool to live in some other country. As long as they don't speak Spanish, of course ..."

"It's near to everything here"

"The best with football? Winning, of course," says Erik Rosling. "Having fun," answers Mathilda Lundblad. For sure, when you combine top division debut with topping the league as she does!

Both of them live in Helsingborg, but about as far apart as you can come geographically – Erik in Hittarp just north of Sofiero and Mathilda on Raus where the city opens up into southern countryside. Though their blocks are about as quiet. The streets meander softly round well-kept, cosy gardens. In Hittarp the Sound glitters blue between modern roof silhouettes and old apple trees. The village clings to the steep edge of the shore ridge and dips its toes into the water in Italianate manner. And to the south Raus climbs cockily to the top of Helsingborg's hillsides to gain a far-flung view over the old Råå hamlet with Ven island on the horizon.

For all that HIF is, in these districts the teams are called Hittarps IK and Råå IF. Both of the youths come from families with football fathers.

Fourteen-year old Erik began to play when he was around seven; Mathilda was a bit older. By fifteen, she was already part of the Råå IF women's team, right now in Division 3 North.

Modestly, but with a gloriously proud smile she says quickly: "It wasn't supposed to happen. I was just going to train with them, but … now I'm part of the team! When I played the first time, I was nervous. I'm the youngest. But with everyone so nice there weren't any problems at all."

To Erik Rosling and Mathilda Lundblad Helsingborg is football – from Hittarps IK in the north to Råå IF in the south.

Stattena IF traditionally dominates women's football in Helsingborg. "They're in Division 1," she explains. But she looks a little sly when she adds: "Right now we're doing great, so you never know …"

Helsingborg likes women's football and who knows, maybe both Eskilsminnes A-team in Division 2 and Stattena need to keep their eyes on the Råå girls in the future?

The clubs are important for both Erik and Mathilda.

"Almost all my mates play Hittarp ball," says Erik. And Mathilda adds: "Yes, there's a lot of football in Helsingborg. New pitches are on the way in several places – Västergård and Rydebäck, for example."

Hittarp boasts of an excellent artificial grass pitch where it's possible to train year-round, says Erik. Much better than gravel, is Mathilda's somewhat jealous response. Both spend many hours on their sport and every minute is worth it. Erik trains several times each week and plays one or two matches ("Sometimes three!"). On Råå Mathilda trains twice a week with the women and once with the girls. She also has two matches per week.

Tough? Yep, not least because there's a lot to do at school. At Högastenskolan where Mathilda is in the ninth class, there are a lot of sports, including a new sports hall. But there are other programs as well, such as media and music. Right now she can't do much more than football and school. In that order if she could choose.

It's great to have a family that loves outdoor life! Here Selma pulls away from master Erik.

"But Daddy always says that school comes first. But I never miss a practice, even if I have a test the next day."

It's a bit calmer for Erik in the Laröd school, at least this year. He doesn't think he has that much homework and does well on the tests without having to study too hard. But what to do when it's time to choose upper secondary direction? No, he hasn't thought that far yet.

"I have no idea what I'll be doing a few years from now. But of course, becoming an athlete is a dream. And then football is fun …"

Mathilda is a year older and will seek upper secondary entry soon, plans to try Natural Science. She thinks about become a doctor. ("Still, I've always wanted to be a marine biologist")

Both like to travel. In the winter there's skiing or snowboard. Mathilda's family travels to Austria, while Erik has been to France. But the snowboard training came a half hour or so from Helsingborg. He and his friends go up to the skiing facility at Våxtorp on the Hallandsåsen Ridge. In the summer, there's always skateboard in the city.

"There's a ramp behind the Dunker Culture Centre where a few of us skate in good weather. I've also sailed a bit, Optimist dinghy, in the Domsten harbour. And the family has sailed on the West Coast and in Denmark. That's OK, but it's even more fun now that I've started riding wakeboard."

"It doesn't matter if there's a lot to do," thinks Mathilda. "If it's fun, it's usually simple."

As a native Rausian, Mathilda is used to having a long way to downtown.

"It does take time to bicycle or take the bus, but it's not far to Råå and most of my friends are there. Nothing against central Helsingborg – I like to stroll on Kullagatan or down in Norra Hamnen – but it's actually just as nice down on Råå!"

"That everything is close to the sea is what I like most about Helsingborg," says Erik and Mathilda agrees. "All you have to do is to jump into the car and you're off and abroad!"

"I really love the sea!"

Kelly Preston – just the name says this is a girl with personality.

"The most important thing is to be yourself! And when I play the drums in a punk band, I feel I'm where I should be."

Kelly is fifteen and lives in Dalhem. She's lived here since she was eight. She was born in Drottninghög and though that's right next-door, it was a big change. Now she laughs a bit about it: "I hadn't been here before, so it felt exciting to be in a new environment."

Kelly thinks living in Dalhem is OK. It's close to the city and there are many buses. Right now it's a quiet Sunday afternoon in the district. Some children are playing between the houses.

"It's quiet here and that's right for me. The neighbours are cool – everybody says hello to everybody. True, there are some who think there isn't much to do here. Many of my friends go downtown, but I'm not a party person. I prefer quiet company. Maybe a backyard grill."

Kelly Preston practicing at the Folkuniversitetet in Gåsebäck. The music centres of several education associations in the area have made it somewhat of a greenhouse for young, new music. One such was the Helsingborg band The Sounds that recorded a demo there in the late 90s.

When she does go into the city, it's with the band. They'll sit a while in the City Park or in the harbour. Or maybe take the ferry to Helsingör and walk around – abroad is just a boat ride away and a youth ticket over and back is only thirty kronor.

"I really love the sea and I have to have greenery around me. Should I move into the city, I'd choose Stattena. There's a park there and it's only five minutes down to the city."

Kelly's Dad comes from Liverpool and last year the family went over to visit with Grandmother and other relatives. It was magic there, says Kelly. Maybe because Liverpool is a port just like Helsingborg.

"I felt right at home! And then the Beatles were Liverpudlians ..."

Music and politics are probably tops for Kelly, except for the family, of course. And they are subjects that involve all of them.

"It was Andy, my brother's friend, who asked if I wanted to be part of Bad Fag. They needed a drummer."

To step into a radical punk band as a fourteen-year old where the oldest member is twenty has meant a lot to Kelly. She thinks in reality she's rather shy. But she's always done things her way. When she came to Dalhemskolan in second grade she was a bit of a tomboy, preferably dressed in her brother Simon's seconds.

"I felt different. The other's didn't understand me. But I've learned not to care that much – that feels good. Otherwise I'd never dared to say yes when Andy asked me to join the band."

Now she practices with Bad Fag twice or three times a week. They play in Gåsebäck where she can borrow drums. What's great with Helsingborg is that there are people with different traditions, she says. "Imagine how dull it would be if everyone was the same!"

Following page:
Storm over the Sound.

49

It started with the Olympics 1834

By Magnus Sjöholm
Sports and culture journalist

A city's sports life always starts with a game. Boys and increasingly girls, meet to play, clubs are formed and grow, more are set up and finally there is a whole flora of associations. That's how it is and that's how it has been ever since sports became organised. Everywhere, worldwide. Well, perhaps not really worldwide. There is a city on the northwestern Scanian coast that did the opposite; put a bit drastically, it started at the goal.

You've heard of Peking –08 and Athens –04. Then there's Helsingborg –34! It's true. Everything started here when Helsingborg's sports life kicked off with the first modern Olympic Games in 1834. Sweden took the national honours from Denmark. There are few reports, but they all agree: the event was a great success! It was held on the old Beridarefältet (the horse-breaker field) that lay about where all ferry-bound cars on their way to Helsingör turn right from the Malmöleden road. That is where the starting block for the modern Olympic Games stood.

Sports researchers don't really agree that the Helsingborg games were the first. Most, including the IOC, think the Athens 1896 or even Stockholm 1912 were the first modern Olympics. But Helsingborg did provide the foundation – if in no other way than that the Stockholm Stadium was built with Helsingborgian "persa-bricks".

After the games, sports life in Helsingborg took a somewhat different direction than in Athens and Stockholm. It is true that the local shooting club was formed the same year as the games were held, but then it took fifty years before the next long-lived club took form in 1883. This was the Helsingborg Rowing Club.

Previous page:
Johan Wissman, running here in IFK Helsingborg's suit on his home track Heden, is one of the world's best 400 metre sprinters.

Moustachioed Danish men

At that point Denmark was at least a year ahead of Sweden when it came to sports from the continent and many were imported through either Helsingborg or Malmö. Younger, moustachioed men (it seemed a requirement) stepped off the boat, were received enthusiastically and moved to some suitable field where the sport was demonstrated. Then the whole thing was rounded out with a traditional banquet, cigars, many lengthy and solemn speeches and the presentation of even grander cups.

The country's first national athletics championships were held in 1896 in the already well-known event city of Helsingborg. In addition to field events, wrestling and football were included and the venue was nearly the same as in 1834.

Olympia, the city's temple of sports, opened two years later in 1898. As the newly formed corporation backing the construction was not allowed to take the name AB Idrott (Sports Inc.), the name of the place where the original games took place was chosen instead. It was planned as a velodrome, a site for cycling, tennis and winter sports – not for football.

In the inaugural speech, Major Andersson pointed out that this was the medicine "against the new national nervousness". He was not completely right. Neither about the nervousness nor about what

The shooting-club's 75th anniversary at Olympia 1908.

Helsingborg IF is the pride of the city and its strongest brand. In the mid-1920s it was called the "Milch cow" – the team raised attendance at all the top division stadiums wherever it played. Its popularity has stayed high through the years.

became the centre for the city's football interested nail-biters.

The shareholder constructions were either passé or a century ahead of itself and betting on velodrome cycling was outlawed. In its place came the modern sports movement as students and workers formed small, not for profit clubs. Most had many sports on their agenda. The Helsingborg Workers' Bicycle and Sports Club usually rode roughshod over the Helsingborg Sports Association (HIF) team in football, but it was the latter that survived. So far Helsingborg has had around 500 different sports associations, of which app. 145 are active today – a number few if any other Swedish city can top.

One of the clubs, specifically Stattena IF, won the first unofficial Champions League title for women. The club was formed in 1922 and played in the men's top league five seasons later. The visit was short, as it was for Råå IF, second-place finisher in 1950-51. This was the HIF's golden era. The club usually had and has so strong an attraction that few other clubs could compete, be it for talent or for space. Until 1957, handball was exiled to Helsingör or Ängelholm or to the "Coal Cellar" at the Berga Barracks.

Sally Bauer was the country's most lauded sports personality during the 30'. Eight days after she had crossed the Kattegat Bay in 17 hours, she danced over the waves from Grisslehamn to Signilskär in Åland in just thirteen hours and six minutes. Her prizes, heavy swimsuits and other paraphernalia can be seen at the Malmö Sports Museum.

Sally chocked the world

During the 20s and 30s swimming across the Sound was a popular sport. The course went from the Helsingör marina to Vikingstrand, which is where the currents usually took the swimmers. One of the watchers was a little girl, the youngest of three swimming sisters. When she was a bit older, she was allowed to join in and then beat both sisters and men. Her name was Sally Bauer and a one-way trip took her around 90 minutes. With the right currents, she would certainly have cut that by a half hour.

Towards the end of the 30s Sally had become the most popular sports personality in Sweden. One reason was that she chocked the male segment by swimming on the same terms as them. Sally swam many long distances, but wasn't sufficiently explosive for the short pool. In a burst of pride over the country's distance swimmers, one Danish company offered a prize to anyone who could break the Danish 29-hour record for crossing the Kattegatt. The prize was five thousand kronor – a fortune at the time. Sally swam the distance and cut the record by some 12 hours!

She followed this by becoming the first Scandinavian to cross the English Channel, the week before WW2 broke out. Well back in Sweden she was feted by a motorcade complete with confetti. The "Sally effect" and the historically strong position swimming had in the city led to the construction of Sweden's handsomest swimming hall. Drawn by Mogens Mogensen, it was inaugurated in 1941.

Classic motor races

The early 30s also saw the start of the large motor races. One hundred fifty thousand persons could come to Landskrona to watch an MC race and the Formula 1 of that period could draw many to the small roads around Norra Vram. The speed was high – too high. There were many accidents, burning houses and one fatal crash. If race secretary Astrid Lindgren had any responsibility for that is unknown. However, one could draw a conclusion from the fact that neither the Emil books, the Noisy Village series, Madicken nor any other of her wonderful stories contain much in the way of motor sports.

Unfortunately the city's motor sport culture has never really got off the ground after the high 30s. The same is true of CK Fix whose cyclists have seldom won on the flat, calm courses of the national championships, perhaps due to the city's hilly topography.

There is, of course, a gigantic exception in Gunnar Nilsson. His meteoric career in the mid-70s led to victory in the Belgian Formula 1 Grand Prix, driving for Lotus, one of the biggest teams of the time. He outshone even Ronnie Peterson and was seen as a real comer. But his career was short. He contracted cancer and died a few months after his Swedish friend and colleague. Gunnar's mother set up a foundation to his memory that gives three million kronor to cancer research each year.

In 1957 the House of Sports – Idrottens Hus – was opened, at that time the largest, most luxurious multi-sport arena in Europe. It had everything. All indoor sports were comfortably accommodated. There was even an exclusive, EVA gym for girls and a stationary four-oar shell so the rowing club could train during the winter.

In the 60s both handball teams won national championships, as did the basketball club. However, when Kalle Svensson retired his goalie gloves, HIF was relegated. Until the team's comeback in the 90s, the city's broad 'alternative' sports life thrived.

The 1950 World Championship match was played São Paolo, but since Rio was easier to say, the goalie hero Kalle Svensson became 'Rio-Kalle' in Sweden. He played 638 elite-level games for HIF. The statue outside Olympia was carved by Risto Karvinen.

Råå BTK were double Swedish Champions during the 2000s, something the men in BTK Rekord have never managed, in spite of their almost permanent elite status.

Nearly 40-years ago IFK Helsingborg dominated Swedish basketball and Jörgen Hansson almost became the first European in the NBA. Today the name of the team is Öresundskraft and is once more in the elite series, but neither Rikard Flink (pictured) nor any other Swede has come any closer to the NBA than Hansson was.

After his eighth European Championship gold in three-cushion billiards, the Expressen evening paper wrote: "A well-dressed man carrying an oblong briefcase meets you among the massed billiard tables in the smoky cellar. He opens his case and assembles his 'weapon'; he's got a hit. As luck would have it, his name is Torbjörn Blomdahl. No lead this time – you'll have to make do with silver, if you're lucky!"

The king of billiards

The tale of father and son Blomdahl started when daddy Lennart set up a billiards hall in the newly built Borgen. The teenage son, Torbjörn, almost needed a stool when he swept the Swedish and later the international elite in three-cushion billiards off their feet. He is seen as the foremost billiards player in all categories. Ever! In the world!

The 70s saw hockey rinks and indoor halls. The city gained an Olympic figure skating princess in Lotta Falkenbäck, but not until after China had chosen to place the 1971 start of its international, so-called ping-pong diplomacy in the small, rather worn outdoor facility on Olympia. Soon thereafter, true capitalism took over and built indoor arenas for both hockey and curling nearby. It is a remarkable feeling that on that chilly Monday evening a few hundred shivering witnesses saw what has now resulted in the Peking Olympic Games 2008.

When later the large ball clubs stopped winning titles, other sports won championships. The Hunter Equestrian Club led by Jan Brink and Peter Eriksson, the gymnastics association and the swimmers had a golden period. For the last, it started in the late 80s and trained by Hans Chrunak, the Helsingborg ladies were perhaps the worlds best for seven or eight years.

IFK Helsingborg was founded in 1895 and has had 22 different sections over the years, including bandy, land hockey, ice hockey and cross-country skiing, focuses no on athletics and a newly formed bobsled section. The patient sprinter Johan Wissman is a concrete result of the club's efforts.

OBL
STADIUM
14
SEM SYSTEM
Del Monte
15
Vikings
TEAM SPORTIK
HD

17

Henrik Larsson: 93 international games, World Championship bronze, winner of the Golden Shoe as the best shooter in Europe, Champions League gold with FC Barcelona, four times league champion in Scotland with Celtic, twice in Spain and in England with Manchester United, HIF-player of the century, twice winner of Sweden's Gold Ball, a member of The Most Excellent Order of the British Empire, honorary doctor at the University of Strathclyde in Glasgow, a born Helsingborgian, married to Magdalena and father to Jordan and Janelle.

However, next to Johan, Henrik Larsson is still the most admired native son. And they are not too different as persons – patient, modest and with a large, frequently expressed love of Helsingborg. This category can also include former football great Roland Nilsson, currently exiled to a managerial job.

Most teams in the top tier

Something else happened around the millennial shift: HIF became the Champions League team from the smallest city ever. At the same time several of the other team sports moved up into the Swedish elite level. Handball and basketball made comebacks, indoor bandy started winning and there were national champions in table tennis, gymnastics, handicap sports and bowling. Variously housed in sports hall cellars, bowling has been more successful than ever during the 2000s, including several European championships. Helsingborg has also trained world-class sportspersons in individual sports such as karate and golf. The latter is rather natural

When the House of Sports was built in 1957, handball benefited. Both the Göta and Vikingarna teams won Swedish Championship titles, while the Olympia team battled in the lower half of the league. Merged, the Olympia/Vikingarna team has moved into the elite series.

In 2007 World Bowling Championship gold went to Helsingborgians Helen Jonsson and Malin Glendorf, together with Nina Falck from Göteborg (right).

Rya south of Helsingborg is one of the many golf courses in the region. In the background you see Öresund and Denmark.

since the Öresund Region has more golf courses than many in the world, with nearly fifty in a 50 km radius from the Stortorget Square. In addition, someone has calculated that Helsingborg has more sports associations at the elite level than any other Swedish city in relation to its size.

Why that's so is hard to answer. One theory is that Helsingborg IF is so dominant that no other association can mature in its shadow. Rather a number of clubs in different sports thrive in this stable, growing region with a rather good economy. The access to halls and training times is also a factor. Though often accused of being stingy, the city is a rather generous in trying to satisfy a seemingly insatiable need.

Add to this that the city's innovative, sports interested politicians have invented something called an "elite grant", a covert support for elite sports. This support is probably grounded on the supposition that if there is no attractive sport on an international level, the city will lack a deep, popular, Helsingborgian breadth.

Certainly an idea that our forefathers seemed to agree with in the Olympic year 1834.

The elite floorball team FC Helsingborg was formed in 2003 when Ramlösa and Högaborg merged. During the winter season, floorball competes with handball and basket for public favour.

The new student life

By Cecilia Attefors
Reporter at the Helsingborg Dagblad

After two years in Helsingborg, Irene Helgesen is convinced, stating without hesitation: "Moving here was the best thing I've done in my life." But it was pure chance that the 22-year old Norwegian woman ended up in Helsingborg and began studying Service Management at Campus Helsingborg.

She's just come back from one of the weeks many training sessions and flops down in the big leather sofa in the living room. Her hair is still moist and her supper stands on the coffee table in front of her. The stereo speakers are hung with medals from Norwegian championships and big cups decorating the bookshelf tell of club records. A collage of pictures dress the wall with Norwegian teammates and family sharing space – next to a photo of her new friends in Helsingborg.

"Running brought me here. I train with IFK Helsingborg, but run for a Norwegian club," she says.

Irene grew up just outside Bergen on Norway's south-western coast. A few years ago she came to a turning point: either stay and study in Norway or move abroad and work on the athletics she'd been part of since she was nine.

"There aren't any indoor tracks in Norway. In Bergen there's a hundred metre track. That's all. But since I run the four hundred, I'd have to move if I wanted to continue, but moving as far away as the States didn't interest me."

Previous page:
Campus Helsingborg was inaugurated in the autumn 2001. Today nearly 3 000 students work in the old Tretorn rubber factory in southern Helsingborg.

Chose Helsingborg

So she looked eastwards towards Sweden. And the choice was between Karlstad and Helsingborg.

"I knew a Norwegian girl who trained here and so it was easier to make contact. And I knew the club had a good coach too."

Still another condition for moving was to be able to study nearby. Naturally she knew that the larger cities had universities and Lund's reputation was international. But she had no idea that it was possible to study in Helsingborg.

"I surfed a bit on Lund's website, looking for the economics program. Then I discovered that you could study in Helsingborg as well. I thought it would be good to have my studies and my training in the same city, so I applied here too."

Lund told her that she'd been placed on the waiting list. But she could start in Helsingborg at once.

"I said yes as soon as I got a place. I didn't even wait to see what would happen in Lund."

By now she's finished two of four years of the Service Management

After lectures, Irene Helgesen and her friends often take a break at one of their many favourites among the city cafes.

program, the largest offered by Lund University at Campus Helsingborg and the first of its kind in Sweden. The university accepts 260 students each year for this program. Size-wise the program is followed by the Sociology and Engineering programs. There are a few additional educational programs and a number of independent courses. In all, there are nearly three thousand students in Tretorn's old rubber factory.

Irene and the other Service Management students are preparing for careers as managers in the service sector and much of the program deals with economy and marketing. The students have four areas to choose from, namely hotel and restaurant, health, tourism and retail trade.

"I'm not disappointed. And that the education is here in Helsingborg is a plus. I'm really happy I didn't study in Lund."

Everything in one place

Even though the Campus is part of Lund University, Irene has all her lectures in Helsingborg. It varies between two and four daily. Most of the students in her program are between twenty and twenty-five years old. About half of them live in Helsingborg, while the rest commute from Malmö, Lund, Halmstad or nearby municipalities.

"The first year we spent a lot of time on campus. This year I've been home a lot. For group work, we've spent time in Lund as well, since several of the girls I work with in the class live there."

After a few visits to the historic educational institution a few kilometres to the south, she sees clear differences.

"Here in Helsingborg everything is in the same place. It's like a large department, in spite of the different subjects. The people are more varied too. The technology, sociology and service management students are all under one roof. It's neat, even if we in fact don't have much to do with each other."

Student stronghold

Lund has always been synonymous with student life, partying, tricks and games. There is a lot of clubbing and something is always happening – many parties and many people.

The question how far behind Helsingborg actually is.

"You can't compare it with Lund. Anyone looking for a full student life, with clubs and everything, will probably be a bit disappointed

Athletics brought Irene Helgesen to Helsingborg.
One of the conditions was that she could study nearby.

here. Student life here is not as intense, though there is always Villan, of course," she explains.

Villan or Consul Persson's villa as it's actually called, is the base for Helsingborg's student life and the social meeting place outside of Campus. The listed house is on Södergatan Street just east of the City Park and a stone's throw from the university. Over the years the house has served as residence for the Consul, office for the city electrical department and home for the municipal music school. Today it's the student's stronghold.

Consul Persson's villa is the student social meeting place, outside of Campus.

The house was renovated in 2003 before the student association Stampus moved in and took over the whole first floor. The house has both assembly rooms and offices. During the day, the Villa serves as café and on Thursdays, the Helsingborg students' traditional night out, the house is turned into a nightclub.

"Just after an exam, it's full. Of course the prices are what draws. A glass of wine is cheaper there than elsewhere and on Thursdays the food is cheap as well. If that was always true, I'd be there all the time," she laughs.

Many of the students start partying at one of the student dormitories and then come to the Villa around eleven for a second pre-party. Then the rounds move on to one of the pubs in the city.

Even if Thursdays and the Thursday pub at the Villa are in a class apart, sometimes there are events on both Fridays and Saturdays.

Sports are demanding

The whole thing is perfect for anyone wanting to get actively involved in student life. Though there's only one club, Stampus has more than the parties. There are sports, chorus and other cultural events.

However, Irene doesn't feel like a typical student. She has training six days a week, sometimes in both morning and evening, and is only fully free on Sundays. Still, don't be surprised if you see her or some of her friends at one of the city cafés – for fika or fiking as Irene says, is a favourite pastime.

"We take coffee breaks all the time, even daily. Most often it's Wayne's, but we go to Fahlman's as well for their yummy cakes. And Ebba's is also a classic."

There are six dormitories in Helsingborg. Most are new or freshly renovated and lie close to campus, but the few square metres are expensive.

Irene was lucky. She lives in a spacious flat in Eneborg she sublets fully furnished. She found out about it the summer before she began studying. A friend of a friend was going to study in Stockholm and wanted to sublet the Helsingborg flat while the studies continued.

"It was perfect timing. Otherwise I would probably have landed in a dorm. Most of my friends live there, but it's expensive for what you get. Socially it can be a lot of fun, but the flats are so small, they're hard to keep neat."

Southern Helsingborg

The Norwegian student support Irene gets is about the same as the Swedish one and it's not fat. When she goes shopping, she often goes to southern Helsingborg.

"Truly a place with development potential. Gustav Adolf market is super. I shop there often since the vegetables are better and cheaper than elsewhere."

Otherwise she has no favourite place in Helsingborg. But she likes living in the southern part of the city.

"It's nice and quiet here. Most everyone I know lives in Eneborg or further south due to campus location and prices. It's nice in the northern parts, but living at Tågaborg would have been a bit far and you'd have been a bit outside."

She was worried in the beginning about coming to a new country and a new city. But that stopped quickly. Once the semester started, the university had mentor weeks for the new students.

"It was great! I felt rather small the first day and there are many who come alone. It's easier at the arranged social bits. Those I spent time with the first weeks are still those I socialize with most now."

Satisfied with her choice

She has no idea how long she'll stay in Helsingborg. But two more years to finish the program is for certain.

"It'll probably be longer. I'm aiming at the European Championships 2010 and the Olympics in 2012 in London."

For a year now she's been part of the Norwegian national team and her time for her 400-metre speciality is the best in Norway this year. The goal is to participate in a European or World Championship or the Olympics. Preferably all three.

"I can't stop now. Moving to Helsingborg is the best thing I've done in my life. If I hadn't, I would have stopped running. And it's great to get away and get to know new people and yourself. I like being a student. It's a free life without so many demands."

Even if the sports plans are carved in stone, the future in her profession is more vague.

"I hope to become a manager. Or have my own company. I don't want to plan too much. There are so many jobs you don't even know about. The management program is good because it includes courses in leadership. But it's a new program and not generally known yet."

Looking back she's still very satisfied having chosen Helsingborg. In much because it's not only students, but a mix with other people as well.

"Campus is close and everything is in one place. For me, it's perfect!"

Scandlines

A step into the Sound

By Lars-Eric Jönsson
Associate professor in ethnology at Lund University

Helsingborg shifts and reaches a bit further into the Sound. The sparkling waters in centre city open gradually to the general public, both for living and leisure. Norra Hamnen was the tryout, where during the 1990s the commercial ship traffic disappeared, along with a complete shunting yard, replaced by attractive apartment houses, a marina and the elongated leisure avenue named Gröningen that stretches towards Fria Bad and Pålsjöbaden.

Today reaching the city's industrial heart calls for long walk south, indeed south of Södern. What we traditionally have seen as the southern district, ranging from Trädgårdsgatan to the Söderviadukt, is today a blend of residences and retail stores. Gåsebäck next door is a colourful mix of small industries and workshops. And west of Söder lies the port area that, together with Gåsebäck, is now the site of Helsingborg's largest city renewal project for many years.

In this the southern harbour the quays are still edged with railway tracks and cranes. There are large parking lots next to spacious warehouses towering by the docks; these, together with the Helsingborg dry dock, have long informed the area. They are all concrete reminders of the port's history and impact.

Previous page:
The southern districts of the city have housed industrial production and transport since the late 1800s. However, the transformation of the Södra Hamnen and on towards Gåsebäck has changed the cityscape radically. Helsingborg steps closer to the Sound and more residents can enjoy the glittering water.

A moveable feast

Surely Helsingborgians have always found pleasure in the Sound and its harbours. But these facilities were designed for shipping sundry goods both inwards and out. In an industrial society the ties between railways and port facilities were especially strong. Indeed, laying rails was frequently matched by building quays. Inaugurated in 1891, Norra Hamnen was laid out as the West Coast Line was built towards the north. The Södra Hamnen was opened in 1880, serving thus the rail line to Hässleholm laid out in 1875. However, the Oceanhamnen had no similar ties to railway construction.

Today the Tretorn premises have kept pace with the times, shifting from industrial to knowledge production.

South of the Södra Hamnen and west of the tracks a number of industries were built between 1880 and 1900, concerns that would be important parts of Helsingborg's commercial life. Among the most important were Sockerfabriken, Galoschfabriken, Helsingborgs varv and Skånska Superfosfat. Farther south a Hussar Regiment was quartered in barracks that today in part house the Rönnowska School. As a whole, the industries, harbours and railways formed a dense and obvious industrial setting that served as a motor for the city's unmatched growth during the late 1800s into the early 1900s.

Today things are different. Following an international trend, industries are moving to the outskirts, a port city process that is mirrored in Stockholm, Göteborg and Malmö – and Helsingborg. From an international perspective London is probably the grandest, most apparent example – if Söder has certain similarities to the East End, Söderhamnen is an analogue to Docklands. This area was the core of London's harbours and shipyards, but as in many European cities, the port grew too small and the yards could not compete with the Asian ones. The Docklands change began in the 1980s and is still ongoing, with many, very large areas awaiting reuse.

It would be wrong to suggest that this is but one of several signs that the industrial society should be dead. It does, however, change and move. In Helsingborg, freight operations using ships and railway cars have moved even further south to the area around Sydhamnen, a move that in no way means that Helsingborg harbour is languishing. Quite the opposite is true, for the city is today one of the leading ports in

northern Europe. In addition to the busy ferry traffic in what is now called Nordhamnen, there is heavy goods traffic in the West, South and Bulk Harbours.

Though not dead, the industrial community has moved. Most of the commercial goods handeld in the harbour has moved further south.

Varied architecture

As said, Södra Hamnen awaits its transformation. For several years now there has been little or no shipping in the docks. Bredgatan is still lined with industrial buildings, but their contents are not as before. The Tretorn factories house education and research within the framework of Lund University. Ikea's main office is in the old sugar factory. New buildings comprising Södra Hamnen, Oceanhamnen and Gåsebäck will surround these buildings.

In order to connect the Söder district with the new harbour district, the railway south of the Knutpunkten hub will be moved underground along several kilometres. The current Malmöleden will become a local street and traffic to the Helsingör ferries and Södra Hamnen will be moved even farther west. This shift of the city's centre towards the

Following page:
Helsingborg also moves west. In order to link the city with the South Harbour area, the railway south will be put in a tunnel. The new area will be dominated by residences and may, as this photomontage illustrates, be organised into blocks and cut by a canal.

Södergatan is the artery of the old Söder district. Will it still be that once the South Harbour district is complete?

south is emphasized by the fact that the Knutpunkten station will be rebuilt with a new railway station and a portal towards the new districts.

The City of Helsingborg is planning for around eight thousand new residences over the next twenty-five years. In addition to these, there will be concomitant retail stores, offices and hotels. It is not yet possible to describe exactly how all this new construction will look. The City Planning Office's sketches suggest a desire to organize the new areas in block-like structures; that is to say, there is a wish to continue the block design and scale from the old Söder district and the existing factory architecture. What will happen to the docks and the water is unclear. Will these areas remain as they are or partially be filled to gain more land to exploit? How close to the water should the buildings stand? What will the balance be between the building's proximity to the water and the general public's access to the same? Quite naturally there are a number of similarly fundamental questions that seek answers, only one of which is how automotive access will shape the area.

From a city planning point of view, Södra Hamnen has several reasons to succeed. The location just west of the current Järnvägsgatan and Malmöleden is exceptionally good, especially when the tracks are laid underground and access to the existing Söder district is facilitated. The city will gain a shoreline that has long been segregated by the railway and the industries. Architecturally there are several alternatives.

During the most recent decades houses with gables facing the street have been built in several cities, a form of Swedish neo-functionalism seen in such places as Stockholm's Hammarby Sjöstad, Malmö's Västra Hamnen and the Norra Älvstranden in Göteborg. But Södra Hamnen is too large to become some sort of pastiche on Norra Hamnen. One alternative presented is to use the brick architecture of the Tretorn factory as inspiration.

However, plans are to extend Södra Hamnen in stages over the course of twenty years and it is neither desirable nor even possible to apply a uniform architecture in such a scale and over so many years. In other words, we can foresee a more varied architecture with many proprietors building over a number of years. This fact will probably turn out to be beneficial for Södra Hamnen. Variation and heterogeneity are the foundation of all city life.

Several city districts

There are even social ambitions for Södra Hamnen. The City of Helsingborg would like to erase the separation of north and south; though this may be more difficult, there are at least some social perspectives here. Class differences cannot be eradicated through construction, but can be shifted in space. The risk is that the current north-south social differentiation will be extended in an east-west direction. Keeping that in mind, it is easy to see that the greatest challenge for the Södra Hamnen transformation is neither architecture nor city planning per se. The question is how to create a new, attractive city area for all Helsingborgians, regardless of income or cultural affinity. Architecture and city planning alone cannot create such an area. What

Söder's heart is Gustaf Adolf Square. There is no other place in Helsingborg with a richer market life than here.

is needed are the economical conditions for people with weaker finances to live in a newly built setting in a much coveted location. That is the true challenge.

Today's Söder district is the most urban in Helsingborg. This does not mean that there are no social problems here, but rather the reverse. Still, though Söder has been maltreated over several decades with comprehensive demolitions and brutal traffic routing, the district has developed a social, cultural dynamic not found elsewhere in Helsingborg. There is more than just ethnic diversity here – there is a mix of trade and other functions that create a social composition. An experiment designed to show this would be to walk down Kullgatan from the north, crossing Stortorget to Södra Storgatan, cross Trädgårdsgatan and follow Södergatan to Gustav Adolf Square. It is not only a journey from north to south. It is also a traverse through the diversity and variation that no other part of the city can offer.

The area around Södra Hamnen, Oceanhamnen and Gåsebäck all own the conditions for contributing to this diversity, not as one new district, but as several. There are some thoughts that the area could serve as a tool for blending Norr and Söder. Perhaps it would be better to let the different city districts keep and develop their unique identities, while the city naturally must work to smooth out those social inequalities that are expressed in the current division between north and south. However, the diversity that is the breath of all large cities ought to be confirmed by expressing the boundaries between its parts without therefore making communication between them worse.

You can glimpse the Sound behind the Furutorpbacken Hill, an unused proximity to the water unused by Helsingborgians in the southern districts.

Södra Hamnen is large and will be important for the city. As this is written, everything is open. But let us hope that the docks, cranes and some warehouse will be allowed to remain, not only to remind us of our past, but also to 'disturb' the new somewhat, in part by creating architectural diversity. Gåsebäck will most likely become a separate city district. It is hoped that some of the small-scale feel will stay and contribute to the area picture in the future too. For it is in the existing and the new, in the people there now and those who will join them that each city district's peculiar nature is born.

Following page:
Fog sweeping in from the Sound. The 1923 goddess statue by Carl Milles was financed by the Malte Sommelius Foundation. The shipping monument was placed on the new Helsingör Quay in 2001 following a thorough renovation.

Photographs

Photographer	Pages
Karl Erik Ander	19
Bildbyrån i Hässleholm	69, 84, 88, 89, 113, 115, 116, 117, 118, 119, 121
Bertil Hagberg/Sesamphoto	12, 22, 24, 26, 38, 71, 72, 73 (below), 75, 130*, 134*
Helsingborgs Dagblad	21, 57, 58, 70, 108, 110, 140
Helsingborgs Idrottsmuseum	112, 114
Helsingborgs Symfoniorkester	48 (above)
Victoria Design	18, 77 (above)
Clas Håkansson	15
Ikea	98
Ole Jais	Back cover, 2, 14, 17, 30 (below), 35, 37, 42, 45, 46, 49, 60, 62, 63, 64, 65 (below), 70 (below), 78, 79, 81, 82, 83, 122, 132, 139
Kulturmagasinet, Helsingborg	16, 74, 77 (below), 80
Pierre Mens	87, 90
Anna-Maria Nildén	52
Tomas Polvall	29, 30 (above), 36, 100
David Skoog	48 (below)
Göran Stenberg	Cover, 6, 10, 11, 23, 31, 32, 34, 40, 50, 55, 56, 65 (above), 66 (below), 68 (below), 73 (above), 76, 86, 92, 94, 95 102, 103, 104, 105, 106, 120, 123, 126, 127, 133, 136, 138
Jörgen Schwartzkopf	66 (above), 67
Sonet	59
Vesna Vrabec	28

* Montage by Cadwalk, Malmö